WordShop

Vocabulary Tools for ESL Students

Intermediate

Phil Stokes
De Anza College

**300+ Focus Words
Over 1,000 Additional Words**

Clip Art courtesy of Corel Corporation.

Cover image by PhotoDisc, 2013 4th Avenue, Seattle, Washington, 98121.

Cover by Phil Stokes

Copyright © 1996 by Phillip F. Stokes

ISBN 0-7872-2377-8

All rights reserved. No part of this publication may be reproduced, stored in a retrieval system, or transmitted, in any form or by any means, electronic, mechanical, photocopying, recording, or otherwise, without the prior written permission of the copyright owner.

Printed in the United States of America
10 9 8 7 6 5 4 3 2

Dedication

**To my parents,
Dick and Barbara Stokes
For their love and support for almost 60 years.**

**To my tiny but loud wife
Ming Huey,
Who has enriched my life in ways I never could have imagined.**

About the Author

Phil with Mom

Phil Stokes has been teaching English at De Anza College since it opened in 1967. Since then, he has taught everything from beginning composition to the Short Story and Linguistics. He created the ESL programs at both De Anza and Foothill Colleges. He taught English 1A in De Anza's first Women's Re-Entry Program. All of his students went on to higher education or employment in good jobs. He taught English in programs for at-risk kids in the Chicano and Black communities and for "white" kids with drug and alcohol problems. Most of these "kids" are now successful in their jobs and in their lives. He was the master teacher in De Anza's Bilingual Teacher Aide program. All of his students were employed as Bilingual Aides upon completion of the program and several are now full time credentialed teachers. These students did the work which produced their success. Phil gave them the tools.

Table of Contents

How to Learn and Remember New Words xi
WordShop: What's In It For You? xiii
How To Use This Book xv
Using the Focus Sheet xix
Using the Study Guide xxi
The WordShop Sound Card xxiii

Chapter 1 1
   Lesson 1 3
      Curly was a cute baby.
   Lesson 2 16
      We never saw him again.
Chapter 2 29
   Lesson 3 31
      Not for all the tea in China!
   Lesson 4 46
      Give me more, more, more!
   Lesson 5 62
      He picked up the office building and threw it into the lake.
Chapter 3 79
   Lesson 6 81
      He'll be late for his own funeral!
   Lesson 7 100
      Senator Foghorn got the floor.
   Lesson 8 118
      I'm not wearing a mask!
   Lesson 9 136
      He used a fictitious name.
Chapter 4 155
   Lesson 10 157
      It slowly fell apart like ancient ruins.
   Lesson 11 176
      She had a lump in her throat.
   Lesson 12 191
      Now that's a paradox.
Chapter 5 205
   Lesson 13 207
      To put it bluntly,
   Lesson 14 224
      Harry is hairy, very hairy.
   Lesson 15 244
      The bunny was attached to the ear.
   Lesson 16 266
      It was what you would call a good plane crash.
Index 283

Preface

WordShop was written with non-native speakers of English in mind, but it also works very well with native speakers who have not yet learned many of the 1,300+ words presented in this book. You can decide whether this book is for you by looking over the Focus Sheets, which you will find at the beginning of every lesson. On these Focus Sheets you will find the focus words - the words that are emphasized in each lesson. You should know some of these. If you find that you know **most** of them, you don't need this book. If you don't know many of the words you see on the Focus Sheets, then you're in for a treat. You get to have some fun learning them. If you don't believe me, just ask my students who have used this book. If you know a focus word, you might want to look at the information given for that word anyway. There's a good chance you'll find words you don't know that are used to explain the focus word you do know. If that's the case, just substitute that word for the one you know, and learn that one. Before you begin, here's a free word for you:

spoof /spuf/ n.

<u>Other forms</u>: spoof /spuf/ v.
<u>Opposite</u>: to be serious with someone
<u>Meaning</u>: If you're spoofing someone, you're having fun with them, you're trying to trick them, you're trying to fool them. You tell them something that is not true, trying to get them to believe it so you can tell them the truth later and laugh with them about how they were fooled. A spoof is a hoax. We tease people after we have spoofed them.

<u>Example</u>:
There are more spoofs on April Fool's Day (April First) than any other day of the year. People all over the western world try very hard to fool their friends, co-workers, classmates, anybody who looks vulnerable. On April Fool's Day, 1996 a full-page ad run in several newspapers told readers that Taco Bell had bought one of the symbols of US independence and renamed it the Taco Liberty Bell.

<u>Example</u>:
The White House was inundated with calls from outraged citizens complaining about the sale of the precious symbol. When someone asked a White House spokesman if it was true, he said yes, that it was part of the government's privatization plans. He said there were plans to sell the Lincoln Memorial to the Ford Motor Company to help pay for repairs. He said the name would, of course, be changed from the Abraham Lincoln Memorial to the Lincoln-Mercury Memorial. I guess the moral of this story is: Complain about a spoof and you get spoofed.

Tip (a little help): **tease** = have fun with someone at his or her expense = kid someone = needle someone
Tip : **vulnerable** = weak = defenseless = unprotected = a sitting duck   continued ▶▶▶

Tip: **inundated with calls** = received many, many phone calls, so many that they could not answer all of them
Tip : **outraged** = (This can be found in *WordShop II*.)
Tip : **precious** = (This can be found in *WordShop II*.)
Tip : **privatization** = paying private companies to do government work or selling government assets (in *WordShop II*) to private companies in return for some benefit
Tip : **moral** = (It's in here someplace.)

So if you knew the meaning of spoof, you could choose any of the words explained in the Word Tips and learn them instead.

A Note for users of <u>Mosaic II: Listening and Speaking</u> *(McGraw-Hill). This book contains vocabulary from the taped conversations and lectures for Chapters 1-5 of the* <u>Mosaic II</u> *text, so* <u>WordShop</u> *is a perfect companion to this text.*

How to Learn and Remember New Words

Here are eight things you can do that will help you learn and remember a new word:

Repetition
Association with Similar Words
Association with Opposites
Association with Personal Experience
Visualizing
Focusing on What You're Learning
Using What You've Learned
Intending to Remember

Let's look at these one at a time.

Repetition refers to memorizing words by repeating them along with their meanings and quizzing yourself on them, or having someone else quiz you on them. It helps if the person quizzing you is this amazingly beautiful (or handsome) person. This is the oldest method around. It is very effective in getting words and their meanings connected in your short term memory. However, if you do only this, you're going to forget many of them.

Associating words with words that have similar meanings puts them in the same mental box. You open one box and you see *happy, joyful, ecstatic, cheerful* and *blissful*. Open another and you see *rich, wealthy, loaded, affluent,* and *opulent*. Open another and you see *crap, dung, guano, manure,* and *feces*. Knowing the meaning of one word in the box helps you remember the others.

Associating words with their opposites helps you learn and remember both. Just knowing a word's opposite deepens your understanding of the meaning of that word. You know the meaning of *difficult*, right? Knowing that *slam dunk* is the opposite of *difficult* automatically tells you what *slam dunk* means. No dictionary needed. That's why you also know the meaning of *facile* when I tell you it's the opposite of difficult. Words can have many "opposites" or none. Obviously, if it has no opposites, this strategy isn't going to help. What is the opposite of *peanut butter*, anyway? You have to look elsewhere.

Associating words with your personal experience, with life events that are familiar to you, or with any crazy thing you can think of also helps you remember them. In fact, the best associations you can make are with things that are unusual, strange, dramatic, or funny. Perhaps you will remember the meaning of the word *putrid* from this story:

One year a teacher friend of mine named Bill Griese bought me a surprise mail order birthday gift. Unfortunately, he didn't realize that I was going to Europe on sabbatical leave for a year and the package arrived at the college about a week after I had left. Dottie, our lovable mail lady, put the package on the shelf above my mailbox. Each month after that another package arrived for me and she put them on the shelf with the others. After five months worth of packages had arrived, people who came into the mailroom began to think that something had died in there. The smell was putrid. Eventually, Dottie discovered that the putrid smell was coming from my packages, so she opened one of them. When she pried the putrid-smelling package open, she discovered a large hunk of limburger cheese. My friend Bill had enrolled me in the Cheese of the Month Club................... You know you've created a strong enough association when the story automatically makes you remember the word and its meaning. As you will see in using this book, learning new words does not have to be boring.

Visualizing obviously helps with words for objects. You can visualize anything that could be a picture or a photograph and, as you know, a picture is worth a 1,000 words. You can also "see" the word itself in your head and connect it with the "picture". **Question**: Do you know what an elf is? **Answer**: No. So you look it up in the dictionary and you get "fairy, fay, sprite, imp, urchin, diminutive spirit, puck, pixy, pygmy." **Response**: Thanks. Now if you really want to know what an elf is, you find a picture of one and take a mental picture of that little critter. That mental picture will pop up when you think of the word and you've got it. Visualizing also helps make associations stronger, so you'll remember them. **Word**: slither. **Association**: The snake slithered along the ground until it stopped against Helen's big toe. **Visualization**: See the Snake. See the snake slither. See Helen's big toe. See Helen about to pee in her pants. You won't forget the association, and you won't forget slither. Visualization can help you condense the association into a **memory sticker**, so that instead of having to recall the entire story, maybe all you need is Helen's big toe.

Focusing on the words you are learning separates them from all the other things that are trying to get your attention. Focusing alone puts them in a special category just like your *Things to Remember* list and your grocery list. Keeping track of your progress helps you keep the focus. It also helps you shorten your list - you cross off words you've learned. As your list becomes shorter, you gain confidence and soon realize that you can actually accomplish what seemed like mission impossible when you started.

If you don't use 'em, you lose 'em. So use the words you've learned in every way you can, so you won't forget them. Read as much as you can, so you can get a sense of how these words are used and a feeling for what words are used with them. Get all your senses involved. See the word. Say the word. Listen to the word as you or someone else say it. Taste the word. Smell the word.

You can only know the real meaning of limburger cheese if you taste it and smell it. (Come to think of it, there are words you just don't want to smell.) Add to your associations as new ones present themselves. Make the word part of the real world. In other words, get it out of the vocabulary book and get it into your life.

Intending to remember means looking the word in the eye and saying, "I'm going to get you. I'm going to remember you. When I call you, you're gonna come. When I need you, you're gonna be there." This may sound kind of stupid, but it works, especially if you imagine a situation where you're going to need this word and you **will** the word to come to you. As you get good at doing this, you'll remember more and more. In fact, getting in the habit of being **determined** to remember words will improve your ability to remember just about anything.
Here's a real life example. One of the reasons I became an English teacher was I hated math. So my life was filled with words rather than numbers, and I was happy. However, one day I was chosen to be the chief negotiator for the teacher's union and I had to go up against a lawyer the school district had just hired to make sure we didn't get much. This lawyer, with all the resources of the finance office, began to snow us with numbers. I had to become an instant budget expert because the union's accountant wouldn't help. So I had to learn, not only what the real numbers were, I had to remember them during negotiation sessions and in presentations to the faculty and the school board. Because it was so important that I get the numbers right, I was **determined** to remember them. For the most part I did, and we got the highest salary increase in the district's history. Being determined to remember those numbers was my secret weapon. And you know what? I'm super at remembering names and phone numbers when I **will** myself to remember them.

WordShop
What's In It For You?

WordShop gives you the tools you need for learning the 300+ words in the book. The words you will learn in **WordShop** are words that are commonly used in college lectures and textbooks. They are not TV quiz show words that are hardly ever used by humans. You won't find *pulchritude* in this book. **WordShop** shows you how these words are pronounced. It suggests how these words are used in sentences. It supplies you with words that have both similar and opposite meanings. It gives you easy-to-understand explanations of the meanings of the words, not cryptic dictionary definitions that are harder to understand than the words you're learning. **WordShop** gives you many examples for each word, and all the examples are in context. In addition, the words are repeated throughout the book.

The examples also provide associations which you can use to remember what the words mean. Moreover, **WordShop** helps you focus on and keep track of what you are learning. So what else do you want?

WordShop also provides plenty of practice with these words, so you not only learn them, but you also remember them long after you have demolished this book. For each of the 16 lessons in this book, you will find pronunciation practice which focuses on stress (very important in English). You will also practice making associations and creating memory stickers from examples given in the book and from events in your own experience. There is practice with word meanings and practice with opposites. There is a real world test asking you whether sentences using each word make sense or not. At the end of each lesson, you have a chance to write your own sentences using the words in the lesson. So what else do you want?

If you buy the **WordShop Tapes** (sold separately), you can hear what you can only see in the book. On tape 1, you will hear the correct pronunciation of every Focus Word and every Word Tip in the book. All the dialogs used in the examples are on tape 2. The longer stories are on tape 3. The **WordShop Memory Cards** (also sold separately) will make your learning portable. They are for quizzing yourself on the bus, during lunch time at work, at the beach (not!). The Focus Word and the Sound Script are on the front side of each card. On the back, you'll find the meaning, example sentences, and a place for you to write in your memory sticker for that word. You will notice that these memory cards are also playing cards, with Jacks, Queens, Kings, etc. of hearts, diamonds, clubs, and spades in the corners of each card, so you can play your favorite card game and indirectly, and without effort, practice your new words at the same time. Instructions for a number of word games are included with the Memory cards, and so is a bonus deck to help you learn the sound symbols more quickly. So what else do you want?

Look for **WordWorks**, the Interactive multimedia version of **WordShop** on CD. **WordWorks** allows you to learn these words and other words at your own pace and at your own skill level. You get only the explanations you need by just clicking on a word. With **WordWorks**, you can instantly get any pronunciation or meaning with the click of a mouse.

Now let's take a closer look at the tools provided in this book.

When you've learned the words in **WordShop**, if you want fun with more words, look for **WordShop II** (published by California English) which contains another 300+ focus words and more than 1,000 additional supplementary words.

How To Use This Book

Each lesson begins with a Focus Sheet. The lessons themselves are divided into two parts: the learning session and the practice session. The learning session consists of six parts: 1. The word, its sound script, and its function label 2. Other forms of the word 3. Opposites 4. The word's meaning 5. Examples and 6. Word tips.

Learning Sessions

---

1. potential /pə.tɛn.shəl/ n.

2. Other forms: **potentially** /pə.tɛn.shəl.li/ adv.
3. Opposite: incapable of doing something
4. Meaning: *Potential* means possibility. If someone has the potential for doing something, that person or something has the ability or opportunity to do it, is capable of doing it, but hasn't done it yet, and may never do it.
5. Example:
   Curly was a cute baby. His sister thought he had the potential to become a cute guy. Sorry Curly.
   Example:
   Charles was 7'4". He certainly had the potential for becoming a professional basketball player, but he never did.
   Example:
   That chemical is potentially dangerous. It can explode if it is exposed to high temperatures.
6. **Tip 1**: Someone or something can have the potential <u>for doing</u> something or the potential <u>to do</u> something.
   Tip 2: potentially is usually used before adjectives: potentially rich, potentially uncomfortable, potentially beneficial, etc.

Pronunciation

The sound script follows each word. Notice that there is a sound script for other forms of the word as well. A sound script contains (1) the sounds of the word, (2) dots which mark the syllables, and (3) a boldface syllable which marks where the strong stress is, the second syllable in potential, above. For each word you are learning, compare the spelling of the word with the pronunciation script. When you do, you may discover that the spelling may not reflect the way the word is pronounced very well. Take *hospital*, for example. Any dummy can see that *hospital* has an **o**, a **p**, and a **t** in it, but it is pronounced /has.bɪ.dəl/. No **o**, no **p**, no **t**. Comparing the pronunciation script with the spelling will show you what to focus on when you are learning to pronounce new words. Then, when you listen to the pronunciation of the word on the **WordShop Tapes**, you'll have a better chance of pronouncing it correctly.

If you don't remember which sound a symbol in the sound script represents, look at the examples on the Sound Card at the end of this section or check it out in the **Sound Deck**, the bonus deck included free with your **WordShop Memory Cards.**

Other forms

You'll find information on some of the word's other forms here, along with their sound scripts. Related words are also found here. These forms perform different functions in sentences. These functions are suggested by the function labels which follow them: n. for nouns, v. for verbs, adj. for adjectives, adv. for adverbs, and rel. for relationals. You get some idea of the range of uses a form has from its function label.

The following sentence illustrates the basic function of verbs: Jack **stomped** on Fred's foot, **whacked** him upside the head, **dug** his fist into Fred's **midriff**, **kicked** him in the teeth, **smashed** him in the nose, and **punctured** his **pimple**. When you look at **foot, head, midriff, teeth, nose,** and **pimple**, you get a sense of how nouns can be used. Even if you didn't know that midriff means stomach, you know that it functions like foot, head, etc. The following sentences show you other functions, or uses, of nouns: Jan kissed Fred. Jane kissed Fred. Rebecca kissed Fred. Zelda kissed Fred. Mary Macaroni kissed Fred. (Actually, it's Mary Marcone.) All the girls are subjects and Fred is the object of their affection. (Makes up for the beating he got from Jack.) The following sentences suggest how adjectives are used: Alice is tall. She's dark. She's intelligent. She's sensitive. She's svelte. If you didn't know that svelte means attractively thin, you still sense that its function in the sentence is the same as tall, etc. Adverbs tell you how, where, when, and how often something is done: George does it gently behind the barn on Friday afternoon every week. **Other forms** are sometimes included in the example sentences and stories so you get a sense of how we use them.

Opposites

The expressions given here are not exact opposites in many cases. Sometimes, exact opposites don't help much (particularly if you never saw them before). The expressions you see here are designed to give you a pretty good idea of the opposite meaning of the word you are learning. There are no opposite words for words which do not have opposites. Remember peanut butter?

Meanings

You will not find 57 totally unfamiliar definitions of the word here, so you can have fun trying to figure out which one fits best. You are given clear explanations of what the word means in the contexts given in the book. These are generally the most frequently used meanings for these words. You will also not find any dead animal parts here. No Latin (a dead language) roots for you to memorize. That's because most of them aren't very helpful for figuring out what modern English words mean.

Examples
The examples are designed to illustrate the meanings of the focus word in sentences. Often the examples are stories or reports or thoughts that are unusual enough to be used as associations for remembering the meaning of the word.

Word Tips
Word Tips give you help with words and expressions used in the examples. They may also give you information necessary for understanding an example. Word Tips allow more "real" examples to be used and they provide you the opportunity to expand your vocabulary well beyond the 300+ focus words in the book. Actually, there are easy-to-understand "definitions" for over 1,300 words in this book.

Practice Sessions

Stress Tests force you to focus on where the strong stress is in each word you are learning. Doing that also helps you remember how to pronounce each word. If you can't pronounce a word, you are not likely to remember what it means. If you stress a word in the wrong place, no one will understand you, even if everything else is OK. That's how important stress is in English.

Associations asks you to make **memory stickers** for each word from the examples given in the book. A memory sticker is a short phrase that reminds you of the example which, in turn, reminds you of the meaning of the word. **Limburger cheese** is a memory sticker for the story told earlier that could help you remember the meaning of *putrid*. Do you remember what it means? **Helen's big toe** is, of course, the memory sticker for *slither*. Do you remember what *slither* means? Many of the examples in the book contain stories or events or insights that provide good material for creating these memory stickers. However, some do not.

Using Your Own Experience gives you the chance to make up your own examples when the examples in the book don't do the trick. Your own personal experience is filled with odd, funny, or gruesome stories that will help you remember the words you are learning. Although it's fun to remember stories that you can use, your memory stickers do not have to be stories. Your memory sticker for **cantankerous** might be your **Aunt Martha** because that's the way she is most of the time. Use these personal memory stickers in place of those you made from the book that didn't work.

Similarities helps you connect words with similar meanings, as simple as that.

Opposites asks you to match opposites with words used in sentences, so you have the context to help you. You are never asked to match lists of isolated words because doing that produces very little long term remembering. Studying lists of isolated words may help you pass a test, but you'll forget everything as soon as the test is over.

Does This Make Sense? tests your ability to use your knowledge of the words introduced in the lesson to make sense of statements and situations. You need to understand and remember what the words in the lesson mean in order to evaluate these statements properly. For a number of the situations, more than one answer may be correct because different interpretations are possible. That's why there's a place for you to explain your answers to some of the test items. In any case, if you are using this book in a class, you will probably be discussing many of these items anyway.

Writing gives you the opportunity to write sentences of your own using the words in the lesson. This gives you additional practice in learning the words and it helps you incorporate the words into your writing. It also gives you more practice with any substitute words you've chosen.

There's no magic to this. Simply follow the instructions for each part and you'll do fine.

Hope you enjoy your time in the WordShop.

Using the Focus Sheet

There is more to learning new words than meets the eye, or ear, nose or throat. Your vocabulary actually consists of four sets of words and expressions. There is a set of words you recognize when you hear them, another set that you recognize when your read them, another set that you use in conversation and discussion, and another you use in writing and in formal speeches. Generally, the recognition vocabularies - the listening and reading sets - are larger than the production set for formal speaking and writing because you can recognize a lot more words than you can produce. For native speakers, the informal conversation set doesn't change much. The reading set is the quickest and easiest to expand. There are two reasons for this: You don't have to produce anything - you only need to recognize what a word means when you read it - and you have an entire context to help you. Getting new words into your formal speaking and writing set takes the most practice because everything has to come from your head. You have to "produce" the word you want without any help. Another reason for this difficulty has to do with the nature of the words themselves. Unlike the conversation set, which consists primarily of native English words which we use all the time, writing and formal speaking require the use of a formal word set, a much higher percent of which have been borrowed from other languages. These are words we do not use often in informal conversations, so we are not as comfortable with them. If English is not your native language, you may have more trouble with the listening and conversation sets than you do with the reading set. My wife said *gimmie pig* for a long time until she saw guinea pig in a book she was reading and asked what it meant. Did you know it was spelled that way? When I was a young college student I walked around pronouncing facade, which I had encountered in a book, as /fə.**ked**/ while assuming the air of the intellectual - until Bonnie Rubenstein, my Humanities professor told me it was /fə.**sad**/. However, for most people, regardless of language background, the formal speaking and writing set is the most difficult to expand.

The Focus Sheet, which begins every lesson in this book, is there to help you get organized. It helps you recognize your starting point and it helps you focus on the kind of practice you need to emphasize in learning these new words. It helps you decide which words you need to work on and recognize which word sets you have the most trouble with.

Lesson 1 Focus Sheet

1	4	2		3		
Word	✔	Subst Word	Listen	Speak	Read	Write
irrational						
trivial						
essential						

You Do Four Things with the Focus Sheet:

1. Look at the list of focus words in the lesson and cross out the words you already know.

2. If you already know a word, look at the info given for it anyway. You might find a word you don't know in the explanation, examples, or Word Tips. If you do find one, write that word in the substitute word column and decide to learn that word instead. If you find more than one word you don't know, add the others to the bottom of the substitute word list.

3. If you can understand or use a word in any of the competency areas, check that competency box.

   Listen = I can understand this word and recognize its meaning when I hear it.
   Speak = I can use this word in conversation.
   Read = I recognize what this word means when I read it.
   Write = I can use this word correctly in my writing.

   You can check the competency boxes later to keep track of your progress as you expand your ability to recognize and use these words.

4. After you have completed the above steps, focus on the words you are going to learn and <u>will</u> yourself to remember them. Put a check after each word as you do this.

Using the Study Guide

The Study Guide at the end of each lesson helps you use all the tools to learn the 300+ focus words and the 1,000 possible substitute words in this book.

Lesson 1 Study Guide

Word	1 Subst	2 Similar	3 Opposite	4 Memory	5 ✓
irrational					
trivial					
essential					

Here's what you do with it.

1. Cross out the words you already know and write in the substitute words you have on your Focus Sheet.
2. Write a word with a similar meaning that helps remind you of the focus word's meaning.
3. Write a word with an opposite meaning.
4. Write your memory sticker here.
5. Put a check in this column when, as you quiz yourself (or others quiz you) on the words in this lesson, you can (1) remember what the word means and (2) you can use it in a sentence.

WordShop II
Sound Card

/b/	bit, bad, boy	/ch/	cheap, chair
/d/	dumb, dead, dog	/ʒ/	pleasure, treasure
/f/	fair, fanny		
/g/	good, god, gold		
/h/	happy, heart	/e/	hey, day, ray
/j/	genuine, judge	/i/	see, me, knee
/k/	crazy, clown	/ai/	hi, fly
/l/	lazy, lake	/o/	dope, boat
/m/	meet, Mary	/u/	rude, mood
/n/	nice, neighbor	/a/	mom, pa
/p/	power, pie	/ɛ/	red, bed
/r/	rug, rat	/ɪ/	it, hit, mit
/s/	safe, sex	/ɔ/	bought, saw
/t/	tap, time	/ʊ/	put, foot
/v/	victory, van	/æ/	fat, cat
/w/	wet, wagon	/ə/	but, rug, cut
/y/	yellow, yam	/oi/	toy, ploy
/z/	zingy, Zelda	/au/	brown, cow
/ŋ/	ring, gong, ding		
/ð/	the, that, this		
/θ/	think, thin	/ər/	her, fur, sir
/sh/	shadow, show		

Chapter 1

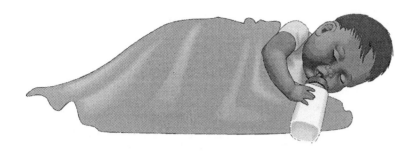

Curly was a cute baby. We all thought he had the potential to be a handsome guy.

Oh well,

Lesson 1 Focus Sheet

Word	✓	Subst Word	Listen	Speak	Read	Write
potential						
gifted						
genius						
temperamental						
considerate						
moody						
loft						
studio						
handle with kid gloves						
disciplined						
artistic						
enthusiastic						
constantly						
boarding school						
drew						
an exception to the rule						

Lesson 1

1. potential /pə.tɛn.shəl/ n.

Other forms: **potentially** /pə.tɛn.shəl.li/ adv. **potential** /pə.tɛn.shəl/ adj.
Opposite: incapable of doing something
Meaning: Potential means possibility. If someone has the potential for doing something, it means that person or something has the ability or opportunity to do it, is capable of doing it, but hasn't done it yet, and may never do it.

Example:
Curly was a cute baby. His sister thought he had the potential to become a cute guy, but he never did. He wasn't ugly, but he definitely wasn't a pretty boy.

Example:
Charles was 7'4". He certainly had the potential for becoming a professional basketball player, but he never did.

Example:
That chemical is potentially dangerous. It can explode if it is exposed to high temperatures.

Tip 1: Someone or something can have the potential <u>for</u> *doing* something or the potential <u>to</u> *do* something.
Tip 2: potentially is usually used before adjectives: potentially rich, potentially uncomfortable, potentially beneficial, etc.

2. gifted /gɪf.təd/ adj.

Other forms: **gift** /gɪft/ n.
Opposite: untalented
Meaning: Gifted means talented. If someone is gifted, he or she has special talents or abilities or skills. We usually think of a gifted person as someone who was born with a talent and then developed that talent. A gifted person has developed that talent to a greater degree than most people, i.e. he or she is better at doing something than most people.

Example:
Charley was a gifted child. He could add, subtract, multiply, and divide when he was only five years old.

Example:
Lemuel is a gifted pianist. He plays the piano better than most people.
Example:
Samuel is a gifted violinist. He plays the violin extremely well.

Example:
George has a gift for writing. He has already published three novels.

Tip 3: musical instrument + ist = the person who plays it (for most instruments).

3. genius /jin.yəs/ n.

Other forms: **ingenious** /ɪn.jin.yəs/ adj. (-ly adv)
Opposite: idiot
Meaning: genius: an extremely smart person; ingenious: a very smart idea

Example:
Charley is a genius. He graduated from the university with a 4.0 GPA when he was twelve years old.

Example:
He could have given the flowers to his girlfriend, but he had a more ingenious idea. He gave them to her mother.

4. temperamental /tɛm.pər.mɛn.təl/ adj. (-ly adv)

Other Forms: **temperament** /tɛm.pər.mɛnt/ n. **temper** /tɛm.pər/ n.
Opposite: easy-going
Meaning: Temperamental, temperament, and temper have somewhat different meanings. Someone who is temperamental gets upset easily. A temperamental person may get angry or irritated or frustrated easily. A person who has a bad temper is someone who gets very angry very quickly. We don't say people have good tempers; we say people have even temperaments. Temperament refers to a person's general emotional state. One person may be generally calm (an even temperament); another may be generally nervous (a nervous temperament.

Example:
Sharon is very temperamental; she gets upset whenever any little thing goes wrong.

Example:
Len has a terrible temper. Last night, he got mad at his wife and threw a chair through their living room window.

5. considerate /kən.sɪd.ər.ət/ adj. (-ly adv)

Other forms: **consider** /kən.sɪ.dər/ v. **consideration** /kən.sɪ.dər.e.shən/ n.
Opposite: not thoughtful
Meaning: A considerate person is aware of people's feelings and needs and acts in a way that takes these feelings and needs into account. We say a considerate person is thoughtful, i.e. he or she thinks of the feelings and needs of others before doing something.

Example:
Nancy is a considerate person; she generally considers the feelings of others; she has consideration for the feelings of others. For example, she always turns the music down when her mom gets home after a long day at work.

Example:
Harry made a lot of noise while his sister was studying for the big exam. He was obviously very inconsiderate.

6. moody /mu.di/ adj.

Other forms: **mood** /mud/ n.
Opposite: happy
Meaning: A moody person changes moods suddenly and is often unhappy. A moody person is in a bad mood more than he or she is in a good mood. A moody person may be dissatisfied, sad, even depressed. However, any of us can be in a bad mood when something "bad" happens to us.

Example:
Joe is quite moody. You never know how he's going to react. Sometimes he's in a good mood, but most of the time he's in a lousy mood. Just the other morning, I said "How's it going?" and he replied, "What the hell do you care?"

Example:
Don't talk to Sally. She's in a bad mood. She just had a fight with her boyfriend.

7. loft /lɔft/ n.

Other forms: **lofty** /lɔf.ti/ adj.
Opposite (of lofty): low
Meaning: A loft is a living or working space in a larger room that is high above floor level and shares the same ceiling as the room. Lofty means high.

Example:
The artist paints in the loft above her family room. When she is done, she climbs down the stairs, goes into the kitchen, and fixes dinner.

Example:
Sharon has a lofty position in the corporation. I think she's the Director of Marketing or something.

8. studio /stu.di.o/ n.

Other forms: **study** /stə.di/ v. **studious** /stu.di.əs/ adj. (-ly adv)
Meaning: A studio is a room for artistic work, e.g. an artist's studio, a music studio. However, a studious person is someone who studies a lot.

Example:
Ann is a music teacher. She teaches her students in her music studio. Ann's husband is a painter. He paints in his studio in the back of the house.

Example:
Gary is a studious person. You can usually find him in the library, back in the stacks.

9. handle with kid gloves /hæn.dəl wɪθ kɪd gləvz/ Idiom

Meaning: If you handle someone or something with kid gloves, you handle them very carefully.

Example:
You have to be careful with temperamental people. They have to be handled with kid gloves.

Example:
These negotiations are critical to the company's future. They must be handled with kid gloves.

10. disciplined /dɪ.sə.plɪnd/ adj.

Other forms: **discipline** /dɪ.sə.plɪn/ n.
Opposite: undiscilined, little self control
Meaning: We say a person who is disciplined is in control of himself or herself. A disciplined person will continue to do what he or she has planned to do even when it is difficult. Discipline is mental training or control that is learned by practice, often by depriving oneself.

Example:
Roger is very disciplined. He has a lot of discipline. He gets up every morning at 5:30 to work on his book, even though there are times when he doesn't want to get up at all.

Example:
Sandy was able to achieve great discipline through meditation.

11. artistic /ar.tɪs.tɪk/ adj. (-ly adv)

Other forms: **art** /art/ n. **art ist** /ar.dɪst/ n.
Opposite: uncreative, artless
Meaning: By definition, artists are artistic because they create art.

Example:
Burt's artistic skill was wasted at General Foods on the design of cereal boxes.

Example:
However, it's difficult for an artist to make a living on his or her art.

12. enthusiastic /ɛn.θu.zi.æs.tɪk/ adj.

Other forms: **enthusiastically** /ɛn.θu.zi.æs.tə.kli/ adv. **enthusiasm** /ɛn.θu.zi.æ.zəm/ n.
Opposite: disinterested, less than enthusiastic = not very excited about something.
Meaning: When someone is enthusiastic about doing something, he or she is excited about doing it. If someone is not enthusiastic about doing something, it may mean that he or she really doesn't want to do it.

Example:
Huey Lin wasn't very enthusiastic about going back to school after being a housewife for twenty years. She didn't have much enthusiasm about returning to school. She was less than enthusiastic about going back. She thought going to school again would be very hard.

13. constantly /kan.stənt.li/ adv.

Other forms: **constant** /kan.stənt/ adj.
Opposite: intermittently
Meaning: Constant activity is continuous, uninterrupted activity. Something that happens constantly may also happen periodically, i.e. from time to time according to some pattern.

Example:
Molly has been coughing constantly since she started smoking again.

Example:
When he was young, Joe was constantly in trouble. It seems like he was always in trouble. He never gets in trouble now.

14. boarding school /bor.dɪŋ skul/ n.

Other forms: **board** /bord/ v.
Opposite (of board): live at home
Meaning: A boarding school is a school where students live, where they reside, while they go to school.

Example:
John lived at the school between the ages of thirteen and eighteen. He saw his parents only on weekends, holidays, and vacations during those years. He boarded at the school. It was a boarding school. He also ate most of his meals at the school. The school gave him **room and board**. Of course, his parents paid for it. They paid a lot for it. Boarding schools are expensive.

15. drew /dru/ v. (past tense of **draw**)

Other forms: **drawing** /drɔ.ɪŋ/ n. **drawn** /drɔn/ adj.
Meaning: to draw means to create a picture or illustration. I draw pictures all the time. In fact, I drew one yesterday. I've drawn many pictures since I was a little boy.

Example:
Betty drew an unusual picture of a goat. It was a goat with a mustache instead of a beard. Can you visualize that goat?

Example:
Billy drew a line in the street and told Sam he would shoot him if Sam crossed it. Good thing it was just an old cowboy movie.

16. an exception to the rule /ɛk.sɛp.ʃən/ n.

Other forms: **exceptional** /ɛk.sɛp.ʃən.əl/ adj. (-ly adv)
Opposite: the way it's usually done
Meaning: An exception is something that does not follow a rule. However, if something is exceptional, it is much better than average.

Example:
Normally, children are not allowed in the pool after 3 PM. However, the apartment manager's grandchildren are visiting from New York today. It is after 3 PM. They are in the pool. When I asked the apartment manager why they were allowed to swim after 3 PM, he said it was an exception to the rule.

Example:
I usually get off work at 5 PM, but tonight is an exception. I have to work until ten.

Practice 1 : Stress test

Directions : If you get the stress in the wrong place, nobody's going to know what the hell you're saying. Underline the loudest syllable.

1. potential 2. gifted 3. artistic 4. disciplined 5. genius
6. temperamental 7. moody 8. enthusiastic 9. considerate
10. constantly 11. boarding school 12. handle 13. studio
14. exception 15. temperament

Practice 2 : Stickers

Directions : Write a memory sticker from a story or example in the book that will help you remember what each word means.

Example: potential : <u>7'4"</u>
       genius : <u>eleven-year-old Charley</u>

1. genius : _____
2. temperamental : _____
3. considerate : _____
4. moody : _____
5. loft : _____
6. studio : _____
7. handle with kid gloves : _____
8. disciplined : _____
9. artistic : _____
10. enthusiastic : _____
11. constantly : _____
12. boarding school : _____
13. drew : _____
14. an exception to the rule : _____

Betty's goat.

Practice 3 : Using Your Own Experience

Directions : Write your own "story". For example, if your aunt Tillie is the smartest person in your family (besides you ,of course) you could write: My Aunt Tillie is a genius. Then you have your own Memory sticker - Aunt Tillie, of course - and you will never forget what *genius* means. If you already know a word, you don't need a memory sticker, so cross it out, write in your substitute word if you found one, and create a memory sticker for that word instead.

1. genius :
_____
_____

2. temperamental :
_____
_____

3. considerate :
_____
_____

4. moody :
_____

5. loft :
_____

6. studio :
_____

7. handle with kid gloves :
_____
_____

8. disciplined :
_____

9. an exception to the rule :
_____

10. enthusiastic :
_____

11. constantly :
_____

12. boarding school :
_____

13. drew :
_____
_____

Practice 4 : Simple Connections

<u>Directions</u> : Choose a word that <u>suggests</u> the meaning of the boldfaced word. Put the appropriate letter in the blank.

a. doesn't follow **b.** draw **c.** reside **d.** continuous **e.** excited **f.** art
g. in control **h.** carefully **i.** painting, music **j.** high **k.** unhappy **l.** thoughtful
m. easily upset **n.** smart **o.** talented **p.** possible

1. The salesman didn't live up to his **potential**. __
2. Fred is only **moody** in the morning before coffee. __
3. He is no **genius**, but he is President. __
4. Sally couldn't paint, but she was **artistic** in other ways. __
5. Lenny was a **considerate** son. He helped his parents a lot. __
6. After six years of college, Gary has no **discipline** left. __
7. Eben had **lofty** ambitions. He wanted to be a millionaire for a living. __
8. Tom is **temperamental**. Every time I mention how beautiful his ex-wife is he gets upset. I don't get it. __
9. Terry is very **enthusiastic** about his new job. __
10. The **boarding school** was home for four years. __
11. Harry **handled** his angry secretary **with kid gloves**. __
12. Sherry **drew** a funny picture of the teacher on the board. __
13. Mr. Ming is the first Chinese to be appointed to the California Supreme Court. We could say he definitely is **an exception**. __
14. Luke is **constantly** getting fired. __
15. Helen is very **gifted**. I hate her. __
16. "Get the hell out of my **studio**," Jerry said to the rat. __

Sally was artistic in other ways.

11

Practice 5 : Opposites

Directions : Choose a word that means the opposite of the boldfaced word. Put the appropriate letter in the blank.

a. happy **b.** disinterested **c.** low **d.** untalented **e.** easy-going
f. incapable **g.** not thoughtful **h.** intermittently **i.** uncreative
j. idiot

1. George has a lot of **potential**. __
2. Tommy is undoubtedly a **gifted** child. __
3. Ivan is certainly a **genius**. __
4. Mary is very **temperamental**. __
5. Joe is quite **considerate**. __
6. Doug is definitely a **moody** person. __
7. The **lofty** clouds drifted slowly by as the day passed. __
8. Monet was obviously **artistic**. __
9. Nancy was very **enthusiastic** about joining the sales team. __
10. Ron **constantly** said the wrong thing in public. __

Practice 6 : Do these make sense, or not?

Directions : If the information in the sentence is consistent, if everything fits OK, if there are no contradictions, nothing improbable or impossible, then write YES in the blank. However, if the parts don't fit, if it doesn't make sense, if its ridiculous or absurd, then write NO in the blank.

1. The salesman didn't live up to his **potential**; he did too much talking and not enough selling. __
2. Sam is certainly a **genius**; he can't even put on two matching socks in the morning. __
3. His wife was not **enthusiastic** when she saw him with another woman. __
4. Shirley is **temperamental**; she needs to be handled with kid gloves. __
5. Harriet received a gold pin from her Dad, so she was **gifted**, right? __
6. Beth quit when she couldn't figure out the math problem after working on it for ten minutes. She was quite **disciplined**. __
7. Nancy always woke Betty up in the morning so Betty wouldn't be late for school. She was very **considerate** in that way. __
8. A **moody** person is unhappy quite a lot. __
9. Kim, who **constantly** complained about her husband at the office, said she loved him very much at family gatherings. __
10. John went to a **boarding school** so he could live away from home. __
11. Jane put the apples and potatoes in the **loft** so they would stay cool. __
12. There were two pianos and a music stand in Ann's **studio**.
13. The architect **drew up** the plans for the new studio last week. __

14. Laura was so artistic that she couldn't draw a straight line. __
15. They let Bill Cosby's daughter into the university even though her grades were not great. University officials said they made an exception to the rule because she had such an interesting personality. They said it had nothing to do with the $1 million Cosby had donated for the new gym. __

Really?
Directions: Explain your answers to these items :

2. _____
3. _____
5. _____
9. _____
11. _____

Write
Directions: Write a sentence of your own for each of the words you are learning. Do not write sentences for words you already know. Instead, write a sentence for any substitute words you have chosen to learn.

Lesson 1 Study Guide

Word	Substitute	Similar	Opposite	Memory	✓
potential					
gifted					
genius					
temperamental					
considerate					
moody					
loft					
studio					
handle with kid gloves					
disciplined					
artistic					
enthusiastic					
constantly					
boarding school					
drew					
an exception to the rule					

Lesson 2 Focus Form

Word	Substitute	Listen	Speak	Read	Write
obedient					
excel					
sympathetic					
projector					
curious					
evolve					
range from X to Y					
insect					
naturalist					
soldier					
although					
jump to conclusions					
excessive					
shy					
encourage					
giant					

Lesson 2

17. obedient /o.bi.di.ənt/ adj. (-ly adv)

Other forms: **obedience** /o.bi.di.əns/ n. **obey** /o.be/ v.
Opposite: disobedient
Meaning: If you obey someone, you do what they tell you to do. When you do, you are being obedient.

Example:
Roy was a very obedient boy; he always obeyed his parents. He did whatever they wanted him to do. In fact, he married the girl his parents picked out for him, even though he didn't like her much.

Example:
He always obeys the law when a policeman is watching.

18. excel /ɛk.sɛl/ v.

Other forms: **excellent** /ɛk.sɛ.lənt/ adj. **excellence** /ɛk.sɛ.ləns/ n.
Opposite: do badly
Meaning: When you excel at something, you do it very well. You do it much better than most other people.

Example:
Sandy excelled in statistics. She got an 'A' in her statistics class even though she had not taken the prerequisite (a class she was supposed to take before statistics). She particularly loved doing spreadsheets, especially Excel.

19. sympathetic /sɪm.pə.θɛ.dɪk/ adj. (-ly adv)

Other forms: sympathy /sɪm.pə.θi/ n.
Opposite: uncaring
Meaning: If I feel sorry for someone because something bad has happened to him, then I have sympathy for him; I feel sympathetic towards him.

Example:
We sent a sympathy card to Mrs. Jamison when we heard that her husband had died.

Example:
When the student who had cheated complained about how difficult the test was, the teacher wasn't very sympathetic with him. I wonder why?

Tip 4: We often use **with** and **towards** when we mention the person we are sympathetic with, e.g. He was sympathetic towards his little brother.

20. projector /pro.jɛk.tər/ n.

Other forms: **project** /pro.jɛkt/ v. **projection** /pro.jɛk.shən/ n.
Meaning: A projector puts an image on a screen or wall.

Example:
The movie projector was broken so, obviously, we couldn't see the movie. Can you believe it? The teacher gave us a test instead.

Example:
Mary placed the slides in the slide projector while people were arriving for her presentation on her trip to Morocco.

21. curious /kyʊr.i.əs/ adj. (-ly adv)

Other forms: **curiosity** /kyʊr.i.a.sə.di/ n.
Opposite: uninterested
Meaning: If you're very curious about something, you really want to know about it. You are very interested in it.

Example:
The young cat was very curious about what was inside the dog house so he went in. We never saw him again.

Example:
The curious little mouse crept onto the Merry-Go-Round just before they started it up. Boy, was he dizzy when the Merry-Go-Round stopped!

22. evolve /i.valv/ v.

Other forms: **evolution** /ɛ.və.lu.shən/ n.
Opposite: change suddenly
Meaning: Things evolve, or change gradually, over time. They do not happen overnight. It takes quite some time for something to evolve.

Example:
Scientists say humans evolved from the apes.

Example:
It's not fair! Lenny says I am an earlier form of evolution. He says I am closer to the apes just because I have lots of hair on my chest.

23. range from X to Y /renj/ Idiom

Meaning: Extending from one point to another. To vary within specific limits.

Example:
The intelligence level of his family ranges from genius to idiot.

Example:
The test scores ranged from a high of 92% to a low of 61%.

Example:
The membership of the California State Assembly ranges from young ambitious kids who know how to win elections, but not much else, to hardened old men who know that only small victories are possible.

Example:
Her taste in men ranges from tall, dark, handsome young "hunks" to short, fat, plain, old men. She does not discriminate. She will take any man as long as he is rich.

24. insect /ɪn.sɛkt/ n.

Other forms: **insecticide** /ɪn.sɛk.tə.saɪd/ n.
Meaning: Insects are small creatures like mosquitoes and flies. Insecticides are poisons which kill insects. (-cide = kill) The informal word for insects is bugs. /bəgz/ The informal expression **to bug somebody** means to bother somebody.

Example:
Bugs are just working class insects.

Example:
Most insects are small, but the cockroaches in the Amazon are bigger than my fist!

Example:
Sherry always bugs me while I'm trying to do the payroll. She keeps talking and talking and it's hard for me to concentrate on the numbers. I bet someday I'm going to issue a monthly check to the janitor for $400,000!

25. naturalist /næ.chʊr.al.lɪst/ n.

Other forms: **nature** /ne.chər/ n. **natural** /næ.chʊr.al/ adj. **naturalism** /næ.chʊr.al.ɪ.zəm/ n.
Meaning: A naturalist is a person who knows a lot about nature and helps to preserve it. Nature is the world the way we found it when humans first appeared on the earth.

Example:
Don't mess with Mother Nature! (Don't interfere with nature's way, or you will pay a price.)

Example:
For most people, a natural environment is more comfortable than an industrial environment.

26. soldier /sol.jər/ n.

Other forms: A more general term is **military** which includes soldiers, sailors, etc.
Opposite: (of military): civilian
Meaning: A soldier is someone who fights in wars or is at least prepares to fight in a war, if necessary.

Example:
Soldiers fight in wars. Some don't come back.

Example:
Military forces have been placed along the common border of Greece and Turkey for some time.

Tip 5: for some time = for quite a while = for a long time

27. although /ɔl.ðo/ Rel.

Other forms: **though** /ðo/ **even though** /i.vən ðo/
Meaning: Although, though, and even though all indicate contrast. Even though provides stronger emphasis.

Example:
She married him even though he didn't have a great job.

Example:
Though he wasn't the smartest, Jerry was the best programmer in the company. He simply worked harder than the smarter guys.

Example:
She didn't say anything, although she thought it wasn't a very good idea.

28. to jump to conclusions /kən.klu.ʒənz/ Idiom

Other forms: **conclude** /kən.klud/ v. **conclusive** /kən.klu.sɪv/ adj. (-ly adv)
Opposite: reach a conclusion after careful thought
Meaning: To jump to conclusions means to reach a conclusion too soon, without enough thought, without enough facts, evidence, information.

Example:
Bob assumed he was going to get the promotion, so he told all his friends about it. However, Susan got the promotion, not Bob. Bob shouldn't have jumped to conclusions about who was going to get the promotion.

Example:
Mary bought the wedding dress because she was sure Bob would ask her to marry him. She shouldn't have jumped to conclusions.

29. excessive /ɛk.sɛ.sɪv/ adj.

Other forms: **excess** /ɛk.sɛs/ n.
Opposite: not too much
Meaning: Excessive means too much.

Example:
Bill Gates has an excessive amount of money. Why doesn't he give some to me?

Example:
The neighbors made far too much food for the neighborhood barbecue. After the barbecue, the excess was given to Anthony's Kitchen, which feeds the homeless.

Example:
Bob often drinks to excess. He frequently finishes a whole bottle of wine with dinner, all by himself.

Tip 6: To do something **to excess** /ɛk.sɛs/ means to do it too much.

30. shy /shai/ adj.

Other forms: **shyness** /shai.nəs/ n.
Opposite: outgoing
Meaning: Someone who is shy is quiet and uncomfortable around other people, usually doesn't talk unless someone speaks to him or her, and doesn't say much even then. Another word for shy is bashful.

Example:
It's OK to be bashful unless your shyness gets in your way.

Example:
Ted was too shy to ask any of the girls to dance.

31. encourage /ɪn.kɚ.əj/ v.

Other forms: **encouraged** /ɪn.kɚ.əjd/ adj. **encouraging** /ɪn.kɚ.ə.jɪŋ/ adj. **encouragement** /ɪn.kɚ.əj.mənt/ n.
Opposite: discourage
Meaning: When you encourage someone, you give them confidence. You tell them they can succeed. You tell them not to give up, not to quit. You tell them they can do it.

Example:
Sandy was ready to quit, but her husband encouraged her to stay in school. He pointed out how well she was doing and he also pointed out that she had only a short time to go before she would graduate.

Example:
Keeping a record of how much I had completed each day encouraged me to finish this book. It gave me a lot of encouragement.

32. giant /jai.ənt/ n.

Other forms: **gigantic** /jai.gæn.tɪk/ adj.
Opposite: dwarf
Meaning: The word giant refers to an imaginary or mythological creature of superhuman size. Sometimes, a very large person, object, or organization is also referred to as a giant. Anything that is gigantic is very, very big.

Example:
David killed the giant by hitting him between the eyes with a stone.

Example:
The giant corporation swallowed up many small businesses.

Example:
The little boy licked the giant ice cream cone for over 20 minutes. When he was done, his Mom cleaned up the large puddle under his chair.

The Merry-Go-Round made the mouse dizzy.

Curiosity killed the cat.

Practice 7 : Stress test

Directions : Underline the loudest syllable.

1. obedient 2. excel 3. sympathetic 4. projector 5. insect
6. curious 7. evolve 8. naturalist 9. excessive
10. soldier 11. although 12. conclusions 13. giant
14. encourage 15. gigantic

Practice 8 : Stickers

Directions : Write a memory sticker from a story or example in the book that will help you remember what each word means.

Example: curious : <u>cat</u>

1. curious : _____
2. evolve : _____
3. range from X to Y : _____
4. insect : _____
5. obedient : _____
6. excel : _____
7. sympathetic : _____
8. project: _____
9. soldier : _____
10. giant : _____
11. jump to conclusions : _____
12. excessive : _____
13. shy : _____
14. encourage : _____

23

Practice 9 : Using Your Own Experience

Directions : Write your own "story" and memory sticker to help you remember these words. If you already know a word, you don't need a memory sticker of course, so write stories or examples only for those words you have trouble with.

1. obedient :
_____
_____

2. excel :
_____

3. sympathetic :
_____

4. project :
_____

5. curious:
_____

6. evolve :
_____

7. range from X to Y :
_____

8. insect :
_____

9. soldier :
_____

10. naturalist :
_____
_____

11. jump to conclusions :
_____

12. excessive :
_____

13. shy :
_____

14. encourage:
_____
_____

Practice 10 : Simple Connections

<u>Directions</u> : Choose a word that <u>suggests</u> the meaning of the boldfaced word. Put the appropriate letter in the blank.

a. obey **b.** do well **c.** feel sorry for **d.** place **e.** interested **f.** bug
g. change slowly **h.** from here to there **i.** fight **j.** but **k.** too soon
l. too much **m.** quiet **n.** help **o.** super big

1. Tim **excelled** on Spanish tests, but when he went to Mexico he couldn't understand anybody. __
2. Ray was too **curious** about the snake and got his hand bitten. __
3. Rose has no **sympathy** for insects. She kills 'em on the spot. __
4. Heather was **shy** until she was ten years old. __
5. Sid's father encouraged him to **encourage** the loan officer to encourage the bank president to give him a loan. __
6. The **giant** was sad because he couldn't find anyone to eat. __
7. The idea **evolved** as he rode home on the bus. __
8. Jim had an **excessive** number of absences, so they fired him. __
9. Don't **jump to conclusions**. This book isn't a piece of cake. __
10. The **soldier** stood by the bombed-out building waiting for the next bomb. __
11. They couldn't find the screen, so they **projected** the movie onto the wall. __
12. Today's temperatures will **range from** a low of 56 to a high of 73. __
13. She was a good cook. The **insects** in her kitchen all weighed at least two pounds. __
14. She loved her little genius **even though** he was temperamental. __
15. His wife taught him to be **obedient**. __

Actually, his wife trained him to be obedient.

25

Practice 11 : Similarities

<u>Directions</u> : Write a word in each blank which has a meaning similar to the words given.

1. although : _____ _____
2. but : _____ _____

Practice 12 : Opposites

<u>Directions</u> : Choose a word that means the opposite of the boldfaced word. Put the appropriate letter in the blank.

a. uninterested **b.** not too much **c.** civilian **d.** discourage **e.** dwarf
f. think first, act later **g.** uncaring **h.** change suddenly **i.** outgoing
j. did badly

1. Tim **excelled** in math, but he did lousy in English. __
2. Tommy is undoubtedly a **curious** child. __
3. Little Lenny has **sympathy** for insects. "No one should be that small," he says. __
4. Mary is very **shy**. __
5. Joe **encourages** his sister to paint. He thinks she'll be a fine artist. __
6. Doug is a **giant**. He's 6'8" and he weighs 390 pounds. __
7. Spring-like weather **evolved** as winter released its hold on the land. __
8. Jo's birthday gift was **excessive**. Her wealthy parents gave her a $3 million house with a three car garage so she would have a place to park the Jag and the Mercedes and the Land Rover they bought her for Christmas. __
9. Nancy **jumped to conclusions** when she assumed they would put her in sales. __
10. Tommy joined the **military** in order to get out of the house. __

Practice 13 : Do these make sense, or not?

Directions: If the information in the sentence is consistent, if everything fits OK, if there are no contradictions, nothing improbable or impossible, then write YES in the blank. However, if the parts don't fit, if it doesn't make sense, if its ridiculous or absurd, then write NO in the blank.

1. The doctor was less sympathetic when he learned that the patient had no money. __
2. The young girl said, "Life is wonderful." "Don't jump to conclusions," said the old woman. __
3. Her boss's excessive criticism made Mary even more shy. __
4. Johnny often did what his Mom told him not to do. He was obedient. __
5. The solution to the problem evolved in just a few seconds. __
6. Jake had no girlfriend because he excelled at romance. __
7. Sam, who lived across the street, projected his picture on Sally's dining room wall so she would not forget him. __
8. The cat would be alive today if it hadn't been so curious. __
9. Tod encouraged his brother to go out for the football team by calling him a weak, worthless wimp. __
10. The soldier picked up his rifle and walked out of the barracks. __
11. My savings range from zero to nothing. __
12. You look at things differently in a re-education camp. For example, you look at insects as dinner. __

Really?
Directions: Explain your answers to these items :

1. _____
2. _____
5. _____
8. _____
10. _____

Write
Directions: Write a sentence of your own for each of the words you are learning. Do not write sentences for words you already know. Instead, write a sentence for any substitute words you have chosen to learn.

Lesson 2 Study Guide

Word	Substitute	Similar	Opposite	Memory	✓
obedient					
excel					
sympathetic					
projector					
curious					
evolve					
range from X to Y					
insect					
naturalist					
soldier					
although					
jump to conclusions					
excessive					
shy					
encourage					
giant					

Chapter 2

He was addicted to alcohol. For him, booze was irresistible. He was hooked on the stuff.

Lesson 3 Focus Sheet

Word	✓	Subst Word	Listen	Speak	Read	Write
white water rafting						
It's settled.						
Not on your life!						
Never in a million years!						
Not for all the tea in China!						
Absolutely not!						
hooked						
irresistible						
disguised						
string						
amateur						
parachute						
pull something off						
infamous						
previous						
disorderly						
sue for damages						
hero, heroine						
delighted						
motivate						

Lesson 3

33. white water rafting /waɪt wɔ.dər ræf.tɪŋ/ Idiom

Other forms: **raft** /ræft/ n.
Meaning: Going white water rafting means getting on a river raft, going downstream until you come to some rapids (places in the river where there are lots of rocks and the current is very swift - fast), and going over the rapids in the raft. A raft is a flat boat with either no sides or very low sides.

Example:
The class went white water rafting on the American River. Going over the rapids was very exciting, but I was glad we got past the rocks without falling out of the raft.

34. It's settled. /sɛ.dəld/ Idiom

Other forms: **settle** /sɛ.dəl/ v. **settlement** /sɛ.dəl.mənt/ n.
Opposite: no agreement
Meaning: To settle means to reach final agreement after some discussion. Occasionally, the expression "It's settled." is used by the person who is trying to convince another person to agree. In this case, it may not mean that the other person has actually agreed. A settlement is an agreement.

Example:
Bill: How much are you selling your History book for?
Dan: Uh, about $15.
Bill: Would you take $10 for it?
Dan: No, but I'll let you have it for $12 - only because I like you.
Bill: OK. That's a deal.
Dan: Now that that's settled, let's go get a pizza at Angelino's.

Example:
The settlement between the grocery chain and the grocery clerk's union was reached after three months of tough negotiations.

Tip 7: We often say we **reach** agreement and **reach** a settlement. We also **arrive at** settlements and agreements.

35. Not on your life! /nat an yor laif/ Idiom
36. Never in a million years!
/nɛv.ər ɪn ə mɪl.yən yirz/ Idiom
37. Not for all the tea in China!
/nat for ɔl ðə ti ɪn Chai.nə/ Idiom
38. Absolutely not! /nat an yor laif/ Idiom

<u>Opposite</u>: Sure. I'd be happy to.
<u>Meaning</u>: All four of the above expressions mean *No! Never! I won't do it!*

<u>Example</u>:
Joe: Will you marry me?
Jane: Not for all the tea in China! You're a jerk. (A jerk is not a nice guy.)

<u>Example</u>:
Henry: Are you going to the Barfington Hotel for dinner tonight?
Phil: Absolutely not! Last time I got sick.

<u>Example</u>:
Mike: Are you going to work for Diamond Dog Biscuit Corporation?
Eben: Are you kidding? Never in a million years! They fired my sister last month for no reason.

<u>Example</u>:
Joan: I'm not going to go out with him! And I'm not going to change my mind.
Bob: Oh come on, he's not that bad!
Joan: You have to be out of your mind! He's a jerk. I wouldn't go out with him for a million dollars. No way. Not on your life. Forget it!

<u>Tip 8</u>: **Are you kidding?** is not a question in this case. It means You've got to be kidding! You've got to be joking! You've got to be out of your mind! (crazy) You can't be serious! That can't be a serious question!

39. hooked on something /hʊkt/ Idiom

<u>Other forms</u>: **hook** /hʊk/ adv.
<u>Opposite</u>: I don't have to have it.
<u>Meaning</u>: Someone who is hooked is addicted to something. A person who is hooked may have an addiction to alcohol, to cocaine, to sex, to excitement, etc. A person is addicted when he or she has to have something, i.e. is unable to avoid it. (Oh by the way, **i.e.** means **that is**.)

Example:
Miranda is hooked on Frank. She won't leave him even though he treats her badly.

Example:
Terry is addicted to alcohol. He's really hooked on booze (alcoholic drinks). He can't stop drinking even though it is ruining his life.

Tip 9: We say someone is hooked **on** something.

40. irresistible /ɪr.rə.zɪs.tə.bəl/ adj.

Opposite: I don't need it.
Other forms: resist /ri.zɪst/ v. resistance /ri.zɪs.təns/ n.
Meaning: If something is irresistible, we can not resist it; we have to have it or we have to do it.

Example:
Although she was on a diet, the eight inch high piece of chocolate cake was irresistible.

Example:
It was irresistible. She couldn't resist telling her know-it-all supervisor that he was wrong.

Tip 10: A **know-it-all** = a person who thinks he or she is always right.

41. disguised /dɪs.gaizd/ adj.

Other forms: **disguise** /dis.gaiz/ v. **disguise** /dis.gaiz/ n.
Opposite: easy to recognize
Meaning: Someone who does not want to be recognized, who does not want to be identified, may wear a disguise. The disguise hides the person's identity.

Example:
The bank robber disguised himself by wearing a blond wig, a dress, and high heels. Actually, he was kind of cute.

Example:
Her real motives were disguised. She pretended to be in love with him, but all she really wanted was his Visa Card.

Tip 11: **wig** = hair piece. **high heels** = high heel shoes

42. to string /strɪŋ/ v.

Other forms: past: strung **string** /strɪŋ/ n.
Meaning: To string usually means to stretch string, rope or wire from one point to another.

Example:
Charley strung the wire from a building on one side of Fifth Avenue to a building on the other side of the street, and then walked across the wire, 44 stories above the busy street to work.

43. amateur /æm.ə.chʊr/ n.

Other forms: **amateurish** /æm.ə.chʊr.ɪsh/ adj.
Opposite: professional
Meaning: An amateur is someone who is not very experienced in something, a beginner, or at least not as experienced as a professional. Amateur athletes are not paid. Professional athletes are paid.

Example:
Lenny was an amateur baseball player while he was in college, but he recently signed a contract with the New York Yankees and now, of course, he's a professional.

Example:
BJ is an amateur boxer. He is hoping to make the US Olympic Team.

Example:
Boss, don't give that complicated job to Ken. His work is still amateurish.

44. parachute /pɛr.ə.shut/ n.

Other forms: **chute** (short form)
Meaning: A parachute is a device used for jumping out of airplanes and not getting your head bashed in when you land.

Example:
The path to misery could be seen in his eyes as he looked down from his parachute at the sharks circling below him in the icy waters of the Pacific.

Example:
Sam had been out of the plane for ten seconds before he realized that he had forgotten to put on his parachute. I bet he remembers next time.

45. pull something off /pʊl/ Idiom

Opposite: to fail
Meaning: If you pull something off, you succeed when you or others think there is little chance of success.

Example:
No one thought Sonny Bono could get elected to Congress, but he pulled it off. He was elected last year, to almost everyone's regret.

Example:
There wasn't much chance that Jack's company would get the contract, but they pulled it off. Amazingly, they beat out IBM to get the contract.

Tip 12: beat out = win over the competition

46. infamous /ɪn.fə.məs/ adj.

Opposite: well known for great accomplishments or good deeds
Meaning: An infamous person is well known, but not for great accomplishments. He or she has a bad reputation. Usually, a person who is infamous is well known for behavior that is unusual and/or unacceptable to the group.

Example:
Lady Godiva is infamous in history because she rode naked through the city on her horse.

Example:
Matthew became infamous when he left the country last month with $10,000,000 of the company's money.

Tip 13: naked = nude = in the buff = wearing no clothes

47. previous /pri.vi.əs/ adj.

Other forms: (-ly adv = previously)
Opposite: later, subsequently
Meaning: previous means earlier. something that came before something else

Example: The committee had to revise the report because the previous version was filled with errors.

Example:
They fought the previous evening over some small matter which kept them apart the whole night. Tonight the moon is dancing in the clear sky. They are in love again.

Tip 14: **error** = mistake

48. disorderly /dɪs.ɔr.dər.li/ adj. ∞ (noun+ly = adj / adj+ly=adv)

Other forms: **disorder** /dɪs.ɔr.dər/ n.
Opposite: neat, orderly
Meaning: disorderly means messy, not neat

Example:
It was an understatement to say that her room was disorderly. It wasn't just disorderly; it was a huge mess!

49. sue for damages /su fɔr dæm.ə.jəz/ Legal Term

Other forms: **suit** /sut/ n. **damage** /dæm.əj/ n. **damage** /dæm.əj/ v.
Meaning: sue = take someone to court. damages = money awarded for a loss of some kind

Example:
After drinking hot coffee and burning her throat at her friend Mary's house, Harriet sued Mary for damages. She asked the court to award her $500,000 because the hot coffee changed her voice. Actually, I like her new voice better than her old one.

Example:
Harriet 's lawsuit definitely damaged her friendship with Mary.

50. hero /hir.o/ heroine /hɛr.o.ɪn/ n.

Other forms: **heroic** /hɛr.o.ɪk/ adj. **heroism** /hɛr.o.ɪz.əm/ n.
Opposite: coward
Meaning: A hero is a courageous man, a man who shows courage, especially when facing danger. A heroine is a courageous woman who does the same thing.

Example:
It was a heroic act for Sally to jump into the river and save the child who was drowning. She is truly a heroine.
Example:
Jack received metals for his heroism in war, but he lost his leg.

51. delighted /də.lai.dəd/ adj.

Other forms: **delight** /də.lait/ n. **delight ful** /də.lait.fʊl/ adj.
Opposite: not happy
Meaning: If you are delighted with something, you are very happy with it. Something which is a delight brings you happiness. If someone is delightful, you enjoy them very much.

Example: Mrs. Geddes' grandchildren are delightful. She delights in seeing them because they are a delight to her and they go home with their parents at the end of the day.

Example:
Sandy was delighted to receive her commission check. It was much bigger than she had expected.

51. motivate /mo.də.vet/ v. (-ate = verb ending)

Other forms: **motivation** /mo.də.**ve**.shən/ n. (-ed/-ing adj = motivated/motivating)
Opposite: discourage
Meaning: You motivate someone when you encourage them to do something they don't think they can do, or they are too lazy to do, etc. People can be motivated in positive and not-so-positive ways. We often motivate ourselves by setting goals we want to achieve.

Example:
Ben's father motivated him to complete college by promising to buy Ben a car when he graduated. Ben graduated. He's now driving the beat up old 1983 Chevy his Dad got him. Hey! His Dad didn't say what kind of car!

Example:
Jim was very motivated when he made the pizza. He knew the poison would finish off his mother-in-law once and for all.

Tip 15: **finish off** = kill = get rid of = wipe out = eliminate = rub out

The infamous pizza.

This is not Sally. This is Lady Godiva.

Practice 14 : Stress test

Directions : Underline the loudest syllable.

1. irresistible 2. disguised 3. amateur 4. parachute 5. hero
6. heroine 7. infamous 8. previous 9. disorderly
10. damages 11. delighted 12. motivate 13. settled
14. motivation 15. absolutely

Practice 15 : Stickers

Directions : Write a memory sticker from a story or example in the book that will help you remember what each word means.

Example: irresistible : chocolate cake

1. It's settled. : _____
2. hooked on something : _____
3. irresistible : _____
4. disguised : _____
5. amateur : _____
6. parachute : _____
7. pull something off : _____
8. infamous: _____
9. previous : _____
10. disorderly: _____
11. heroine : _____
12. delighted : _____
13. motivate : _____
14. sue for damages : _____

Practice 16: Using Your Own Experience

Directions: Write your own "story" and memory sticker to help you remember these words. If you already know a word, you don't need a memory sticker, of course, so write stories or examples only for those words you have trouble with.

1. It's settled. : _____
_____

2. hooked on something : _____
_____

3. irresistible : _____
_____

4. disguised : _____
_____

5. amateur : _____
_____

6. parachute : _____
_____

7. pull something off : _____
_____

8. infamous : _____
_____

9. previous : _____
_____

10. disorderly : _____
_____

11. heroine : _____
_____

12. delighted : _____
_____

13. motivate : _____
_____

14. sue for damages : _____
_____

Practice 17: Simple Connections

Directions: Choose a word that <u>suggests</u> the meaning of the boldfaced word. Put the appropriate letter in the blank.

a. rapids **b.** agree **c.** no **d.** addicted **e.** have to have it **f.** hidden
g. stretch **h.** not paid **i.** jump **j.** succeed **k.** bad reputation **l.** earlier
m. messy **n.** take to court **o.** courage **p.** very happy **q.** encourage

1. Paul couldn't **pull it off**. He lost the election by a few votes. __
2. **Amateur** baseball players drink free beer after the game. __
3. Tom was **motivated** to apply for the new position after his co-workers suggested it. __
4. The union and the company **settled** on a 5% salary increase. __
5. The **heroine** stood beside the **hero** waiting for her metal. __
6. Ann had a **disorderly** mind. She had trouble organizing her thoughts. __
7. The $250 green dress that was on sale at 70% off was **irresistible**. __
8. **Previously**, he was poor. Then he created a CD ROM game. __
9. Neil is **hooked on** thin blondes with fat purses. __
10. ---
    Dick: I locked myself out of my office again.
    Jane: **Disguise yourself** as a worm and crawl in though the keyhole. __
11. Prince Charles and Princess Diana are **infamous**. __
12. Cy went **white water rafting** on the American River. __
13. ---
    Jane: Are you going to the dance?
    Dick: **Not on your life!** I can't dance. Are you?
    Jane: No, I can't dance either.
    Dick: Well then, why don't we go to the Drive-In and make out? (make out = kiss and things) __
14. The linemen **strung** the phone lines from pole to pole. __
15. Angie hung a **parachute** from the ceiling above her bed. __
16. Eben was **delighted** when they wanted him to be a TV producer. __
17. Bill **sued** the insurance company because it would not renew his earthquake insurance. __

Practice 18 : Similarities

Directions : Write a word in each blank which has a meaning similar to the words given.

1. Not on your life! : _____ _____ _____
2. Are you kidding? : _____ _____ _____ _____
3. naked : _____
4. error : _____
5. finish off : _____ _____

Practice 19: Opposites

Directions : Choose a word that means the opposite of the boldfaced word. Put the appropriate letter in the blank.

a. no agreement **b.** I don't have to have it. **c.** I don't need it.
d. easy to recognize **e.** professional **f.** fail **g.** later **h.** neat **i.** coward
j. discourage

1. Tim **pulled it off.** He finally climbed Mt. McKinley. __
2. Fanny is an **amateur** skydiver. __
3. Terry was **motivated** to stand by the tack Mary had placed on his seat. __
4. It's **settled**. __
5. Cathy was truly a **heroine**. She saved her mother'-in-law's life. __
6. Doug's room was **disorderly** unless his girlfriend was coming over. __
7. A swimming pool on a hot summer's day is **irresistible**. __
8. Mel is a lawyer now. **Previously**, he was in jail. __
9. Nancy is **hooked on** frozen yogurt. __
10. Last Halloween, Tracy was **disguised** as Napoleon's mother-in-law. __

Practice 20 : Do these make sense, or not?

Directions : If the information in the sentence is consistent, if everything fits OK, if there are no contradictions, nothing improbable or impossible, then write YES in the blank. However, if the parts don't fit, if it doesn't make sense, if its ridiculous or absurd, then write NO in the blank.

1. **Amateurs** and **professionals** are both paid too much. __
2. Heather had trouble with her **disorderly** class. __
3. Ben and Jerry's Chunky Monkey ice cream was **irresistible**. __
4. People who are afraid of heights simply **delight** in **parachuting**. __
5. Money **motivates** politicians to vote for just about anything. __
6. Jake's **previous** job was so easy it was difficult. __
7. He was a **heroine**. __
8. She hurt my feelings so bad I'm thinking about **suing for damages**. __
9. Tod's **hooked on** alcohol; when he drinks even a little, he gets sick. __
10. ---
    Sue: I'm not going to Hawaii, and that's final!
    Bill: OK then **it's settled**. I'll get your ticket for Hawaii tomorrow. __
11. The cake was so **irresistible** that Hank threw it in the garbage. __
12. Well, they **pulled it off**. They didn't finish the project on time. __
13. Hey! Let's go to the desert and go **white water rafting**. __
14. ---
    Stranger: Hey! You want a million bucks, buddy?
    Dan: **Not on your life!** Not for all the tea in China! Never in a million years. I wouldn't touch it with a ten foot pole. __
15. Madonna is **infamous**. So is Rose Anne. __

Really?
Directions: Explain your answers to these items :

6. _____
10. _____
14. _____

Write
Directions: Write a sentence of your own for each of the words you are learning. Do not write sentences for words you already know. Instead, write a sentence for any substitute words you have chosen to learn.

Lesson 3 Study Guide

Word	Substitute	Similar	Opposite	Memory	✓
white water rafting					
It's settled.					
Not on your life!					
Never in a million years!					
Not for all the tea in China!					
Absolutely not!					
hooked					
irresistible					
disguised					
string					
amateur					
parachute					
pull something off					
infamous					
previous					
disorderly					
sue for damages					
hero, heroine					
delighted					
motivate					

Lesson 4 Focus Sheet

Word	✔	Subst Word	Listen	Speak	Read	Write
prosecution						
stunt						
thrill						
fundamental						
sensation						
seek						
greedy						
theorize						
risky						
anxious						
intense						
mental						
long for something						
avant guarde						
hippie						
swinger						
optimal						
boredom						

Lesson 4

52. prosecution /prɑ.sə.kyu.shən/ n. (-tion = noun ending)

Other forms: **prosecute** /prɑ.sə.kyut/ v. (-ed/-ing adj)
Meaning: The legal system prosecutes someone when it takes them to court and attempts to prove they are guilty. The government's lawyer is the prosecuting attorney, while the defendant's lawyer is the defense attorney.

Example:
"The prosecution rests."

Example:
Ken was prosecuted for car theft and drug dealing.

Tip 16: the prosecution = the government's case; case = presentation at a court trial; rests = is finished
Tip 17: drug **dealing** = selling drugs

53. stunt /stənt/ n.
Other forms: **stunt man/ stunt woman** n.
Meaning: A stunt person is someone who performs stunts - usually for money, but sometimes just for the excitement. A stunt is a dangerous or unusual act performed in public to impress the people who are watching.

Example:
A stunt man pulled out his gun and shot another stunt man who was standing on the roof of the old building. The second stunt man fell off the roof, did a somersault in the air, and landed in the hay, to the delight of the Universal Studios audience. The adults thought it was a good stunt; the children thought the second stunt man was dead - until he got up and waved his hat to the audience.

Tip 18: horses eat **hay**; You do a **somersault** when you jump into the air and turn your body all the way around in the air before you land on the ground.

54. thrill /θrɪl/ n.

Other forms: thrill /θrɪl/ v. thrilling /θrɪl.ɪŋ/ adj.
Opposite: boring
Meaning: Something exciting. A thrilling experience is an exciting experience.

Example:
The Super Bowl was filled with thrills. Jerry Rice catching the 80-yard pass in the end zone was the biggest thrill for 49er fans.

Example:
The water ride at Great America is very thrilling.

55. fundamental /fən.də.mɛn.təl/ adj. (-al = adj. ending)

Other forms: **fundamentally** /fən.də.mɛn.təl.li/ adv.
Meaning: fundamental means basic. Fundamentally and basically have about the same meaning.

Example:
Opening the flower shop in that terrible location was a fundamental mistake. Cupertino Florist was out of business in only six months.

Example:
Freedom of speech is a fundamental right of all Americans, but I wish he would shut up..

56. sensation /sɛn.se.shən/ n.

Other forms: sense /sɛns/ v. **sensational** /sɛn.se.shən.əl/ adj.
Opposite: numbness
Meaning: Sensation means feeling. We feel when we sense something with our senses - seeing, hearing, touching, smelling, and tasting. Sensational is not usually used to refer to the senses; it usually means "great", "terrific", "wonderful".

Example:
She felt a strange sensation. When she looked down, she saw the snake wrapping itself around her leg.

Example:
She sensed that the interviewer was more interested in her body than her brains.

Example:
The boss thought Sarah's report was sensational, so he gave her a raise right on the spot.

Tip 19: We often say that some people have **a sixth sense**: They are able to sense another person's feelings even when they are not expressed. They may have a feeling that something is going to happen, before it happens.
Tip 20: **right on the spot** = right away and right there = immediately

57. seek /sik/ v.

Other forms: **sought** /sɔt/ (past tense) v.
Opposite: don't try to find
Meaning: To seek means to look for, search for. When you are seeking something, you are trying to find it. Seek is quite formal.

Example:
Malcom was seeking only peace and quiet when he tripped on the gold bar sticking out of the sand on the beach. He got more than he was looking for.

Example:
Elizabeth Taylor sought happiness in marriage. When she didn't find it in one, she tried another. That's why she's had so many husbands.

58. greedy /gri.di/ adj. (-y often = adj. ending)

Other forms: **greed** /grid/ n. **greediness** /gri.di.nəs/ n.
Opposite: generous
Meaning: Give me more, more, more! Greedy people always want more. They are never satisfied with what they have. Greed and greediness have the same meaning. Greed is a little bit more formal.

Example:
Kathy was very greedy. She said she would only marry a rich man. She also said she would marry a very rich man even if she didn't like him!

Example:
Kathy's greediness led to her unhappiness.

59. theorize /θi.ər.aiz/ v. (-ize = verb ending)

Other forms: **theory** /θɪr.i/ n. **theoretical** /θi.ər.rɛ.də.kəl/ adj.
Meaning: To theorize means to develop a theory. A theory is a possible explanation of why something happened or why something happens the way it does. We only theorize when we don't know for sure why something happened. It's an educated guess.

Example:
Police investigators theorized that the bank robbery was an inside job because there was no sign of breaking and entering.

Example:
One disproved theory is that the earth is flat.

Example:
His belief that he could make a lot of money in the stock market was only theoretical since he never had enough money to invest in the market.

Tip 21: **an inside job** = someone working for the bank committed the crime; breaking and entering = breaking into the bank by force, e.g. shooting off the lock or breaking down the door. (Holy mackerel! I forgot to tell you that **e.g.** means **for example**.)

60. risky /rɪs.ki/ adj.

Other forms: **risk** /rɪsk/ n.
Opposite: safe
Meaning: Something that is risky is dangerous in some way.

Example:
The soldier risked his life trying to save his friend.

Example:
Talking to the boss the way she did was pretty risky; she could have lost her job.

61. anxious /æŋ.shəs/ adj.

Other forms: **anxiety** /æŋ.**zai**.ə.ti/ n. (-ly adv)
Opposite: calm
Meaning: A person is anxious when he or she is nervous or worried about what may happen. Some people are in a continuous state of anxiety; they are always nervous and fearful about what might happen. However, when we say a person is anxious to do something, anxious has a different meaning. It means the person wants to do it very badly.

Example:
Clara was very anxious about her job interview. She was afraid she wouldn't do very well.

Example:
Joe was so worried about his business that he put himself into a state of anxiety that was so bad that he couldn't work at all, which made matters worse, of course.

Tip 22: **fearful** = afraid = scared
Tip 23: **make matters worse** = make things worse

62. intense /ɪn.tɛns/ adj.

Other forms: **intensity** /ɪn.tɛns.ə.ti/ n. (-ly adv)
Opposite: mild
Meaning: intense means very strong

Example:
The father's anger was intense when he saw that big girl hit his little daughter.

Example:
They were all caught up in the intensity of their work just before the deadline.

Tip 24: **deadline** = the time the work had to be done

63. mental /mɛn.təl/ adj.

Other forms: **mind** /maind/ n. (-ly adv)
Opposite: physical
Meaning: Anything mental is related to the mind, to thinking, rather than doing.

Example:
Mental images of his wife danced before him as he sat against the high wall of the prison camp.

Example:
Her pain was mental, not physical, so they sent her to a psychiatrist.

64. long for something /lɔŋ for/ v.

Other forms: **longing** /lɔŋ.ɪŋ/ n.
Opposite: I don't want it at all.
Meaning: If you long for something, you want it very badly. Longing is the feeling we have when we want something very badly, but can't have it.

Example:
Leroy longed to be with his girlfriend, who had moved away from California to go to college in Florida.

Example:
Pat longed for the days when he was young and healthy.

65. avant garde /a.vant gard/ adj. (French)

Opposite: behind the times
Meaning: avant garde means ahead of, usually ahead of what is acceptable at any given time, something new and different.

Example:
Henry definitely didn't like avant guarde music and he didn't like avant guarde painting. He was comfortable with 1940's big band music and paintings of children with dogs.

Tip 25: any **given** time = any specific time = any particular time

66. hippie /hɪ.pi/ n.

Other forms: **hip** /hɪp/ adj.
Opposite (of hip): unaware
Meaning: Hippies were the 1960's and 1970's flower children whose favorite slogans were "Make love, not war" and "Question authority". To be hip means to be aware of the latest and most avant guarde music, fashions, verbal expressions, etc.

Example:
Yesterday's hippies are today's BMW-driving business executives.

Example:
There are some commercial hippies doing business on Telegraph Avenue in Berkeley, but we don't know if they ever saw a flower.

Tip 26: **slogan** = saying

67. swinger /swɪŋ.ər/ n.

Other forms: **swing** /swɪŋ/ v.
Meaning: The word swinger is usually used to refer to single men who go around chasing girls and having "a good time". To swing means to have a good time, usually dancing, drinking, etc. To a swinger, the purpose of life is to have fun.

Example:
Wilt Chamberlain was a swinger in his younger days. He used to have a large mirror on the ceiling above his bed.

Example:
Swingers are known for avoiding commitments and deep feelings.

68. optimal /ap.tə.məl/ adj.

Other forms: **optimum** /ap.tə.məm/ n. **optimize** /ap.tə.maiz/ v.
Opposite: worst
Meaning: If something happens under optimal conditions, it happens under the best conditions.

Example:
They got married under optimal conditions. They had both finished their education. They both had good jobs. They had known each other for several years. They knew each other's bad habits and they still loved each other.

Example:
Jerry tried to optimize his chances of winning the lottery by buying 200 tickets. Not too smart when the odds are 14,000,000 to 1.

69. boredom /bor.dəm/ n. (-dom = noun ending)

Other forms: **boring** /bor.ɪŋ/ adj. **bored** /bord/ adj. **bore** /bor/ v.
Opposite (of boring): thrilling
Meaning: If you are filled with boredom, you are very bored. You are not at all interested in what is going on. Typically, you wish you were somewhere else because life is dull.

Example:
The class was boring, and I didn't need it for graduation, so I dropped it. I was so bored I couldn't stand it another day.

Example:
The air was filled with boredom as the speaker talked on and on into the night.

Example:
Obviously, the speaker bored the audience.

Charles is a perfect match for Kathy.

Practice 21 : Stress test

Directions : Underline the loudest syllable.

1. prosecution 2. stunt 3. fundamental 4. sensation 5. thrill
6. boredom 7. greedy 8. theorize 9. anxious 10. seek 11. risky
12. intense 13. mental 14. long for something 15. hippie 16. swinger 17. avant guarde 18. optimal

Practice 22 : Stickers

Directions : Write a memory sticker from a story or example in the book that will help you remember what each word means. Cross out the words you already know and concentrate on those you don't.

Example: greedy: <u>Kathy</u>

1. prosecution : _____
2. stunt : _____
3. thrill : _____
4. fundamental : _____
5. sensation : _____
6. seek : _____
7. greedy : _____
8. theorize : _____
9. risky : _____
10. anxious : _____
11. intense : _____
12. mental : _____
13. long for something : _____
14. avant guarde : _____
15. hippie : _____
16. swinger : _____
17. optimal : _____
18. boredom : _____

Practice 23 : Using Your Own Experience

Directions: Write your own "story" and memory sticker to help you remember these words. If you already know a word, you don't need a Memory sticker, of course, so write stories or examples only for those words you have trouble with.

1. prosecution :

2. stunt :

3. thrill :

4. fundamental :

5. sensation :

6. seek :

7. greedy :

8. theorize :

9. risky :

10. anxious :

11. intense :

12. mental :

13. long for something :

14. avant guarde :
_____
_____
15. hippie :
_____
_____
16. swinger :
_____
_____
17. optimal :
_____
_____
18. boredom :
_____
_____

Practice 24: Simple Connections

Directions: Choose a word that <u>suggests</u> the meaning of the boldfaced word. Put the appropriate letter in the blank.

a. take to court b. public act c. excitement d. basic e. feeling
f. look for g. not satisfied h. educated guess i. dangerous j. nervous
k. strong l. mind m. want badly n. ahead of o. aware p. fun q. best
r. dull

1. It wasn't the **optimal** time to introduce his new girlfriend to his boss. He couldn't remember her name. __
2. Heather is never too **anxious** about auditions. She's determined. __
3. All too often in business, **greed** is king. __
4. Phil did not have a **thrilling** time in the hospital having back surgery. __
5. Little Lenny **longed for** a pet rat. __
6. There was **intense** pressure on the team to win. __
7. There was no **sensation** in his leg after the surgery. __
8. Taking that job was a bit **risky**. __
9. That's a rather **avant guarde** tie, George. A fish with an umbrella? __
10. Henry is **seeking** the glasses that now sit atop his head. __
11. Prince Charles and Princess Diana getting married was a **fundamental** mistake. __
12. Cy broke his political neck trying to pull off the **stunt**. __
13. **Boredom** is preferable to pain. __
14. My **theory** is that, since we have proven that the moon is not made of green cheese, Venus must be made of green cheese. __
15. Juan should be **prosecuted** for theft. He has stolen too many hearts. __
16. Juan's friend Dick was also a **swinger**. __
17. It was a **mental** error. He threw the ball to a guy on the other team who then raced down the court and dunked to win the game with no time left on the clock. __
18. If he was anything, the jazz musician was **hip**. __

Practice 25 : Similarities

Directions : Write a word in each blank which has a meaning similar to the words given.

1. right on the spot : _____ _____ _____
2. fearful : _____ _____ _____ _____

Practice 26 : Opposites

Directions : Choose a word that means the opposite of the boldfaced word. Put the appropriate letter in the blank.

a. boring b. numbness c. don't try to find it d. generous e. safe
f. calm g. mild h. I don't want it at all i. behind the times j. worst

1. The **optimal** time to climb Mt. McKinley is in the summer. __
2. Heide was very **anxious** about her exams. __
3. Ben was very **greedy**. He could never make enough money. __
4. Since they got married, life was a **thrill** a minute. __
5. Cathy **longed for** the day when her mother-in-law would leave. __
6. The atmosphere was **intense** as they played Ma-Jong for Paul's wife. __
7. I'm sure there is no **sensation** in his brain. __
8. Being honest can be **risky**, but it's worth the risk. __
9. Fred always took an **avant guarde** approach to business. __
10. Barbara was **seeking** employment as a credit manager. __

Practice 27 : Do these make sense, or not?

Directions : If the information in the sentence is consistent, if everything fits OK, if there are no contradictions, nothing improbable or impossible, then write YES in the blank. However, if the parts don't fit, if it doesn't make sense, if its ridiculous or absurd, then write NO in the blank.

1. It's true that he was filled with **greed**, but he didn't care much about money. __
2. Ted's wife **longed for** the opportunity to clean the toilet. __
3. Joe **theorized** that the piece of fruit in front of him was an apple. __
4. Helen found what she **sought**, so she is seeking it later. __
5. The **optimal** time for getting a suntan is between 1 a.m. and 3 a.m. __
6. The **intense** pain didn't bother him much. __
7. Taking **risks** can be dangerous. __
8. Valerie was **thrilled** that she passed her French final. __
9. There was a **fundamental** change in his attitude after he became King. __
10. Nell's going to be **prosecuted** for stepping on a frog. __
11. Feeling a strange **sensation** on her head, Janet looked in the mirror to see if her hair had gotten out of place and discovered the lizard sitting there staring at her. __
12. Bill was **anxious** to leave the room because he had to go to the bathroom, bad! __
13. I don't want to hear any more of those old-fashioned **avant guarde** ideas! __
14. The Yankee fan was filled with **boredom** with the score tied in the bottom of the ninth, bases loaded, two out, a three-two count on the batter, and the pennant on the line. __
15. Hal is a **swinger**. He sits around his apartment all weekend waiting for something to happen. __
16. Jo broke her leg so they took her to a **mental** hospital. __
17. Ippy was aware of what was going on; he was really **hip**. __
18. The **stunt man** got paid for crashing cars into buildings. __

Really?
Directions: Explain your answers to these items :

3. _____
9. _____
10. _____
13. _____

Write
Directions: Write a sentence of your own for each of the words you are learning. Do not write sentences for words you already know. Instead, write a sentence for any substitute words you have chosen to learn.

Lesson 4 Study Guide

Word	Substitute	Similar	Opposite	Memory	✓
prosecution					
stunt					
thrill					
fundamental					
sensation					
seek					
greedy					
theorize					
risky					
anxious					
intense					
mental					
long for something					
avant guarde					
hippie					
swinger					
optimal					
boredom					

The snake wrapped itself around Tom as a sign of affection. Tom wishes it weren't so affectionate.

Lesson 5 Focus Sheet

Word	✔	Subst Word	Listen	Speak	Read	Write
repetition						
routine						
variety						
considerable						
tend to						
pattern						
particularly						
adolescent						
most likely						
extraordinarily						
remarkably						
unusually						
extremely						
reasonable						
creativity						
nonconformity						
dominance						
extroversion						
guts						
popularize						
foolish						

Lesson 5

70. repetition /rɛ.pə.tɪ.shən/ n.

Other forms: **repeat** /ri.pit/ v. **repeatedly** /ri.pit.əd.li/ adv.

Opposite: one time only
Meaning: repeating means doing the same thing more than one time.

Example:
She repeatedly threatened to divorce him; then one day she just walked out of the house and never came back.

Example:
Repetition can be boring.

71. routine /ru.tin/ adj.

Other forms: **routine** /ru.tin/ n. (-ly adv)
Opposite: unusual
Meaning: Routine things are things we do very often, for example daily or weekly. We do them so often that we don't think about them much.

Example:
Even the most exciting job can become routine. We need to find ways to keep it interesting.

Example:
Sam is routinely late for work. I don't know how long he's going to be able to keep his job.

72. variety /və.rai.ə.ti/ n.

Other forms: **vary** /vɛr.i/ v. **various** /vɛr.i.əs/ adv. **variant** /vɛr.i.ənt/ n.
Opposite: the same old thing
Meaning: Variety refers to differences. When you have a lot of different types of things in the same category, you have variety. When things vary, they are different from each other in some way.

Example:
There was a variety of fruit in the large bowl. There were cherries and bananas and grapes and apples. There were even some kiwis and papayas.

Example:
There were various kinds of stones in the river. One day, I found a small piece of jade.

Example:
You have to be careful with June. Her mood varies from moment to moment.

73. considerable /kən.sɪd.ər.ə.bəl/ Quantity Expression

Opposite: not much
Meaning: Considerable means **a lot**.

Example:
Tim has considerable experience in mountain climbing. He's already climbed five of the highest mountains in the world.

Example:
Edgar has a considerable amount of money in the bank. Pretty soon, he'll have enough to buy a fairly (sort of, kind of) large house.

74. tend to /tɛnd tu/ v.

Other forms: **have a tendency to** /tɛnd.dɛn.si/ v. **tend towards** /tɛnd tordz/ v. **tendency** /tɛnd.dɛn.si/ n.
Meaning: Whenever I have a tendency to do something in a certain situation, I have an inclination to do it; I lean in the direction of doing it; I will probably do it instead of something else.

Example:
Lee tends to get nervous around cats; she was scratched by one when she was a baby.

Example:
Unfortunately, Paul has a tendency to perspire (sweat) around beautiful women.

Example:
Society tends towards chaos when there are weak leaders.

Example:
Some tendencies are harmless; some are harmful. Harmful: The tendency to pick fights with guys who are twice your size.

75. pattern /pæt.ərn/ n.

Other forms: **patterned** /pæt.ərnd/ adj. **pattern after** /pæt.ərn/ v.
Meaning: A pattern is a design or model. Patterns usually contain repetitions of elements (parts). Patterns are often used for decoration. The verb to pattern after means to imitate (copy) something or someone.

Example:
The patterns on the walls of the Mosque are amazingly beautiful.

Example:
The pattern for the US flag consists of stars and stripes.

Example:
Phil patterned himself after his father in some ways and his mother in others. He built bedrooms like his father and planted roses like his mom.

76. particularly /pə.tɪk.yə.lər.li/ adv.

Other forms: **particular** /pə.tɪk.yə.lər/ adj.
Opposite: generally
Meaning: particularly means especially

Example:
The President was angry at the Senate for not supporting him on the budget, but he was particularly angry at Senator Clayhead because Clayhead had said earlier that he would support the President.

Example:
In general, I like beans, but I don't like these particular beans because they are overcooked.

77. adolescent /æ.də.lɛ.sənt/ n.

Other forms: **adolescence** /æ.də.lɛ.səns/ n.
Meaning: When we talk about an adolescent, we usually mean a young person between puberty and adulthood.

Example:
Adolescence is often a very confusing time for adolescents and a very irritating time for their parents.

Example:
Three adolescents walked into the 7-Eleven and bought "cardboard" hamburgers again.

Tip 27: puberty = the age at which a person has the ability to produce babies
Tip 28: Notice that adolescence and adolescents are pronounced in the same way: /æ.də.lɛ.səns/.
Tip 29: "cardboard" = like cardboard. These marks (" ") mean don't take the word literally. In this case, the hamburgers are not really made of cardboard; they just taste like it.

78. most likely /most laik.li/ adv.

Other forms: **liklihood** /laik.li.hʊd/ n.
Opposite: least probable
Meaning: If something is most likely to happen, there is a very high probability that it will happen, i.e. it probably will happen.

Example:
Bob Dole was the most likely Republican candidate for the Presidency.

Example:
There is a strong likelihood that a big earthquake will hit Los Angeles in the next thirty years.

Example:
It is highly unlikely that Sonny Bono will be elected President of the United States.

Tip 30: If it probably won't happen, we often say it is **unlikely** to happen.
Tip 31: We sometimes use **a strong** and **little** with likelihood to add emphasis: There is a strong likelihood that something will happen. There is little likelihood that something will happen. (Notice that we do not use **a** with little in this case.)
Tip 32: **highly** unlikely = very unlikely

79. extraordinarily /ɛks.stror.dən.ɛr.ə.li/ Intensifier
80. remarkably /ri.mark.ə.bli/ Intensifier
81. unusually /ən.yu.ʒe.li/ Intensifier
82. extremely /ɛk.strim.li/ Intensifier

Other forms: **uncommonly** /ən.ka.mən.li/ Intensifier (formal)
Meaning: all these mean **very, very**

Example:
The giant in the story was extraordinarily strong; he picked up the office building and threw it into the lake.

Example:
The eleven-year-old boy was remarkably intelligent. He got an 'A' in Zoology. I got a 'C'. I hated him.

Example:
Jamie was uncommonly depressed after he learned that he didn't get the part in the movie.

Example:
Sometimes my brother is extremely stubborn. He will not change his mind even when I prove he is wrong.

83. reasonable /ri.zən.ə.bʊl/ adj.

Other forms: **reason** /ri.zən/ v. **reason** /ri.zən/ n. **reasonableness** /ri.zən.ə.bʊl.nəs/ n.
Opposite: unreasonable
Meaning: Reasonable means logical. If something is reasonable, it makes sense.

Example:
The price was reasonable, so I bought the wooden banana tree this morning in Bali. Now I have to figure out how I'm going to get it back to the States.

Example:
His unreasonableness was only exceeded by his stupidity.

Example:
We reasoned that the product would be successful if we could get it to market before the competition.

Tip 33: If we are talking about prices or expenses, reasonable means **not too high**. The verb **to reason** means to think. The noun **reason** means the explanation (or excuse) for why we did something.
Tip 34: **figure out** = determine = think of a way to do something
Tip 35: **exceed** = greater or bigger than
Tip 36: **stupidity** = being really stupid
Tip 37: **get to market** = make a product available for purchase
Tip 38: **purchase** = buy

84. creativity /kri.ə.tɪv.ə.ti/ n. (-ity = noun ending)

Other forms: **create** /kri.et/ adj. **creative** /kri.e.tɪv/ adj. (-ive = adj. ending)
Opposite: uncreative
Meaning: Creativity may include creating or inventing new things or coming up with new ideas or it may mean doing things in a new and different way. Creativity refers to the process of being creative.

Example:
Bigfoot isn't especially creative. In fact, I'd say he hasn't had an idea for years. Besides, he keeps leaving the same footprints all over the place.

Example:
If we were paid according to our creativity, most artists would be millionaires and most finance officers would be paupers.

Tip 39: **pauper** = a very poor person

85. nonconformity /nan.kən.for.mə.ti/ n.

Other forms: **nonconformist** /nan.kən.**for**.mɪst/ n.
Opposite: doing what others do
Meaning: A nonconformist is a person who generally refuses to do things the way the group does. A nonconformist resists following the crowd. Nonconformity is the behavior exhibited (shown) by a nonconformist.

Example:
That teenager with the purple and green hair is a nonconformist; all of the other teenagers in her group have orange and blue hair.

Example:
By itself, nonconformity does not mean independence. It often means simply conforming to a different standard. That's why all those teenagers who are trying to be different from their parents have earrings in the same places.

Tip 40: **generally** = usually = typically = commonly

86. dominance /dam.ən.əns/ n. (adj. with -t endings very often become nouns with -ce endings)

Other forms: **dominant** /dam.ən.ənt/ adj. **domination** /dam.ən.**e**.shən/ n.
dominate /dam.ən.et/ v.
Opposite: submissiveness
Meaning: Dominance means complete control over others.

Example:
The Kansas City Chiefs have dominated the Oakland Raiders in the last five years. They have beaten them every year and they have beaten them badly.

Example:
Mrs. Smith dominates her husband; she always tells him what to do and how to do it - and, you know what? He does it just the way she wants it.

87. extroversion /ɛk.strə.vər.ʒən/ n.

Other forms: **extrovert** /ɛk.strə.vərt/ n. **extroverted** /ɛk.strə.vər.dəd/ adj.
Opposite: introversion, introverted
Meaning: An extrovert is an outgoing person who likes to be around people and likes to talk. An introvert, on the other hand, tends to be shy, doesn't like to have a lot of people around, and doesn't like to talk much. We usually use these terms to refer to people who are extroverts or introverts in some obvious way, since we all tend to be either extroverted or introverted in some situations.

Example:
Sam certainly is not an extrovert. His idea of a party is to have his mom over for tea.

Example:
My daughter Heather is quite an extrovert. She can get on an elevator with a couple of strangers on the first floor and by the time they have reached the eighth floor she's been invited to their summer cabin for a week and they want to introduce her to their son.

88. guts /gəts/ n. (Informal)

Other forms: **gutsy** /gət.si/ , **gutty** /gə.ti/ adj.
Opposite: cowardice, cowardly, 'chicken'
Meaning: Someone who has guts, or nerve, has the courage to do something that is daring or risky.

Example:
That was really a gutty performance! Jackson played the whole game with a broken rib.

Example:
Can you believe that? Jack had the guts to ask me for another $20! He's owed me $50 since last year and he hasn't even tried to pay me back.

Tip 41: Something is **daring** if few people are willing to do it because it could be dangerous or embarrassing.

89. popularize /pap.yə.lə.raiz/ v.

Other forms: **popular** /pap.yə.lər/ adj.
Opposite: make unpopular, create a dislike for
Meaning: Popularize is a somewhat old-fashioned word which means to make something more popular, i.e. to encourage lots of people to like something or do something.

Example:
Annette Funicello and the other Musketeers helped to popularize the hula hoop.

Example:
The Windows operating system has become very popular even though the Macintosh operating system is much better and much easier to use.

90. foolish /fulˈɪsh/ adj. (-ish is often an adj. ending)

Other forms: **fool** /ful/ n. **fool hardy** /fulˈ.har.di/ adj. (formal)
Opposite: smart
Meaning: A fool is a stupid person. When someone acts foolishly, he or she is being stupid at that time.

Example:
It was very foolish of Sharon to make a promise she couldn't keep.

Example:
It was foolhardy for Sylvester to think he could become President of the club; nobody liked him.

Example:
Gene was a damn' fool! After he spent all his money on that gal, she ran away with the bartender.

Pam was particularly knowledgeable about chickens.

Practice 28 : Stress test

Directions : Underline the loudest syllable.

1. repetition 2. routine 3. variety 4. considerable 5. pattern
6. particularly 7. adolescent 8. extraordinarily 9. remarkably
10. unusually 11. extremely 12. reasonable 13. creativity
14. nonconformity 15. dominance 16. extrovert 17. introvert
18. popularize 19. foolish

Practice 29: Stickers

Directions : Write a memory sticker from a story or example in the book that will help you remember what each word means. Cross out the words you already know and concentrate on those you don't.

Example: nonconformity: purple and green hair

1. repetition : _____
2. routine : _____
3. variety : _____
4. considerable : _____
5. tends to : _____
6. pattern : _____
7. particularly : _____
8. adolescent : _____
9. most likely : _____
10. extraordinarily : _____
11. remarkably : _____
12. extremely : _____
13. reasonable : _____
14. creativity : _____
15. nonconformity : _____
16. dominance : _____
17. extroversion : _____
18. guts : _____
19. popularize : _____
20. foolish : _____

Practice 30 : Using Your Own Experience

Directions : Write your own "story" and memory sticker to help you remember these words. If you already know a word, you don't need a memory sticker, of course, so write stories or examples only for those words you have trouble with.

1. repetition :
   _____
   _____
2. routine :
   _____
3. variety :
   _____
4. considerable :
   _____
5. tend to :
   _____
6. pattern :
   _____
7. particularly :
   _____
8. adolescent :
   _____
9. most likely :
   _____
10. extraordinarily, remarkably, extremely, unusually :
    _____
11. reasonable :
    _____
12. creative :
    _____
13. nonconformist :
    _____
14. dominate :
    _____
    _____

15. extrovert:
_____
_____
16. introvert:
_____
_____
17. guts:
_____
_____
18. popularize:
_____
_____
19. popularity:
_____
_____
20. foolish:
_____
_____

Practice 31 : Simple Connections

Directions : Choose a word that <u>suggests</u> the meaning of the boldfaced word. Put the appropriate letter in the blank.

a. repeat **b.** often **c.** differences **d.** a lot **e.** especially **f.** probably
g. resist **h.** control **i.** outgoing **j.** courage **k.** inclination **l.** design **m.** stupid
n. teenager **o.** very, very **p.** logical **q.** inventive **r.** make popular

1. Mike's **dominance** over his wife made us uncomfortable. __
2. **Repetition** is one form of practice. __
3. Elaine was **particularly** uninformed about slugs. __
4. Ted looks **considerably** older than I do. __
5. The **nonconformists** parachuted down to the altar where they were married a few minutes after they had landed. __
6. I hate **routines** . Give me variety any day. But parachuting to your wedding? That's a bit much! __
7. Where's Lenny? He's **most likely** at the lake pretending to fish. __
8. **Extroverts** tell jokes. __
9. **Variety** is the spice of life. __
10. You have to have **guts** to survive these days. __
11. The chickens **tend to** get anxious when the weather is bad. __
12. It's **foolish** to leave the keys in the car when you pay for gas. __
13. Sherry was pretty **reasonable** when Gary explained why he was two hours late for their date. She hit him only three times. __
14. Sid paid an extra $2,000 for the **pattern** painted on the Transam. __
15. **Adolescents** should be kept in a cage until they are adults. __
16. Betty is very **creative**. She put this sign above the toilet for the guys in the house: Be Real Sweet. Before you retreat. Put down the seat. __
17. Bill Gates spent a lot of money **popularizing** Windows 95. __
18. I am **remarkably** intelligent. And humble. __

Practice 32 : Similarities

<u>Directions</u> : Write a word in each blank which has a meaning similar to the words given.

1. uncommonly : _____ _____ _____ _____
2. figure out _____
3. purchase _____
4. daring _____

Practice 33 : Opposites

<u>Directions</u> : Choose a word that means the opposite of the boldfaced word. Put the appropriate letter in the blank.

a. one time only **b.** unusual **c.** the same old thing
d. not much **e.** generally **f.** least probable **g.** doing what others do
h. submissiveness **i.** introversion **j.** cowardice

1. Mike's **dominance** over his secretary was sickening to watch. __
2. **Repetition** is necessary for remembering. __
3. Elaine was **particularly** knowledgeable about chickens. __
4. She has **considerable** skill in breeding them. __
5. Nine-year-old Kevin was a **nonconformist**. He didn't mind soap. __
6. It was a pretty **routine** job. Stick out your hand. Take the money. Wait for the next car. __
7. What was that? Don't worry. It was **most likely** just a ghost. __
8. Jan's a real **extrovert** when she drinks. She dances on pianos. __
9. The person in number 6 could use some **variety**. __
10. Eilis has a lot of **guts**. She asked the boss to double her salary. __

Practice 34 : Do these make sense, or not?

Directions: If the information in the sentence is consistent, if everything fits OK, if there are no contradictions, nothing improbable or impossible, then write YES in the blank. However, if the parts don't fit, if it doesn't make sense, if its ridiculous or absurd, then write NO in the blank.

1. Sue finally had the **guts** to divorce her abusive husband. __
2. Paul was a **nonconformist**. He was the only one in the group who refused to drink and drive. Five years later, he was also the only one alive. __
3. Ben was so **dominant** that his friends were a little afraid of him. __
4. An **extrovert** hates to be around a lot of people. __
5. It's **foolish** to lock your doors and windows at night. __
6. All this **repetition** is enough to make you sick. __
7. Students **have a tendency to** sleep in early morning classes. __
8. Geometrical **patterns** are orderly. __
9. **Adolescents** love to be around adults. __
10. For **variety**, we had peanut butter sandwiches every day. __
11. —
    Helen: We're missing a fork.
    Dick: **Most likely**, one of the guests threw it in the garbage. __
12. The 5'7" basketball player was **extraordinarily** tall. __
13. An elephant is **considerably** larger than a mouse. __
14. It was unreasonable to divide the pie in quarters for the four people. __
15. The Beatles were quite **popular**. __
16. It's difficult to be **creative** after a long, hard day at the office. __
17. There's less **routine** when the kids are home during the summer. __

Really?
Directions: Explain your answers to these items :

6. _____
9. _____
12. _____
14. _____
17. _____

Write
Directions: Write a sentence of your own for each of the words you are learning. Do not write sentences for words you already know. Instead, write a sentence for any substitute words you have chosen to learn.

Lesson 5 Study Guide

Word	Substitute	Similar	Opposite	Memory	✓
repetition					
routine					
variety					
considerable					
tend to					
pattern					
particularly					
adolescent					
most likely					
extraordinarily					
remarkably					
unusually					
extremely					
reasonable					
creativity					
nonconformity					
dominance					
extroversion					
guts					
popularize					
foolish					

Roy sells a lot of computers, but he is something of a non-conformist.

Chapter 3

I am a liberal conservative standing foursquare in the middle of the road.

Lesson 6 Focus Sheet

Word	✓	Subst Word	Listen	Speak	Read	Write
infancy						
condolence						
rite						
ritual						
funeral						
transition						
frightening						
stressful						
relieve						
role						
dramatic						
maturation						
spectrum						
subtle						
isolation						
on a single occasion						
origin						
to coin						
evident						
transformation						

Lesson 6

91. infancy /ɪn.fənt.si/ n.

Other forms: **infant** /ɪn.fənt/ n. **infantile** /ɪn.fən.tail/ adj.
Opposite: old age
Meaning: An infant is a newly born baby. Infancy is the period of time when one is an infant. If something is in its infancy, it has just begun. If someone acts in an infantile way, they are acting like a baby.

Example:
I was dropped on my head when I was an infant. That explains why I am the way I am today.

Example:
My company is still in its infancy, so we cannot predict how well it will do.

Example:
It was certainly infantile of him to throw his report on the floor and walk out of the meeting after it was criticized by members of the committee.

92. .i.condolences /kən.dol.ən.səz/ n.

Other forms: **console** /kən.sol/ v. **consolation** /kan.sol.e.shun/ n.
Meaning: We offer our condolences when someone has lost a loved one. When we do that, we tell the person how sorry we are that their loved one has died. Sometimes, we offer condolences to others when something terrible has happened to them. We try to console them, i.e. we try to help them feel better.

Example:
Hal offered his condolences to Mary after her husband Bill had died.

Example:
Kim tried to console Jane after she failed the state nursing exam, but there was no consolation in the world that could have made Jane feel better.

Tip 42: We **give** or **offer** condolences.

93. rite /rait/ n.

Other forms: **ritual** /rɪ.chu.əl/ v.
Meaning: Rites are formal ceremonies or practices which symbolize an important event in a society. Many rites are associated with religion and have symbolic meaning for those who participate in them.

Example:
Rites of passage are ceremonies which mark a change from one stage in life to another. Puberty rites, for example, mark the change from adolescence to adulthood.

Example:
Puberty rites in some cultures include separation from the primary group for a period of time.

Tip 43: **adulthood** = the sometimes frustrating condition being an adult.
primary = main = basic

94. ritual /rɪ.chu.əl/ n.

Other forms: **ritually** /rɪ.chu.əl.li/ adv.
Meaning: Rituals are the particular acts or practices which make up a rite or ceremony. These acts or practices are repeated each time the ceremony is performed. The word ritual is also used for any type of repeated behavior.

Example:
When I was a child, the Communion rituals in the Roman Catholic Church consisted of the following: The priest blessed (prayed over) the hosts, or wafers, walked to the altar rail where the people were kneeling, and placed a wafer on the tongue of each person who was waiting to receive it.

Tip 44: The people in charge **perform** the rituals; the others **participate in** them.
Tip 45: **wafer** = /we.fər/ a very thin slice of bread or cracker

95. funeral /fyun.rəl/ n.

Meaning: Funeral services are rites which mark a person's death. Quite often, they also symbolize the passage of the person's spirit into another world. They also commemorate (help people remember) that person's life.

Example:
A number of family members and friends got up to speak about Bill's life, about what he meant to them, about how he had helped them, about the humorous things he had done. Every word they spoke at the funeral showed their love for him.

Example:
Sam is late for everything. I bet he'll be late for his own funeral!

96. transition /træn.zɪ.shən/ n.

Other forms: **transitional** /træn.zɪ.shən.əl/ adj.
Opposite: lasting, permanent
Meaning: A transition is a period of time between stages or events.

Example:
Joel didn't do much during his summer breaks from college classes. He saw them as merely transitions between one year of agony and another.

Example:
Adolescence is often a confusing transition between childhood and adulthood.

Tip 46: **merely** = only = just

97. frightening /fraɪt.nɪŋ/ adj.

Other forms: **fright** /fraɪt/ n. **fright en** /fraɪt.ən/ v.
Meaning: If something is frightening, it is scary; it makes you frightened, afraid, scared.

Example:
When the first big aftershock hit only twenty minutes after the earthquake had destroyed their house, they were filled with fright.

Example:
Boy, that earthquake was a frightening experience. It frightened the hell out of us! Edgar was really afraid, too. I tell you, we were all scared to death!

Tip 47: We say people are **filled with** fright.
Tip 48: **scared to death** = very frightened

98. stressful /strɛs.fʊl/ adj.

Other forms: **stress** /strɛs/ n. **stressed out** /strɛst aʊt/ adj. (informal)
Opposite: calm
Meaning: People who are under stress feels lots of pressure because of the demands of their lives.

Example:
Working for Mr. Johnson was a very stressful experience for Sally because he was such a demanding boss. He gave her too much work to do and he always wanted things done yesterday.

Example:
Obviously, Sally was very stressed out on her job. That's why she quit. Nobody can take that much stress for long.
Tip 49: **want something done yesterday** = want it done before it is possible to get it done
Tip 50: **take stress** = put up with stress = endure stress = live with stress
for long = for a long time

99. relieve /ri.liv/ v.

Other forms: **relieved** /ri.**liv**d/ adj. **relief** /ri.**lif**/ n.
Opposite: under stress
Meaning: We are relieved of stress when the stress goes away, when we are removed from a stressful situation. We are also relieved when something we are worried about doesn't happen. We may also feel relieved when something we were worried about does happen, but it wasn't as bad as we thought it would be.

Example:
Betty's mom was pretty worried when Betty wasn't at school when she went to pick her up. She was relieved when Betty called an hour later to say she had gone to her friend's house.

Example:
Her mom was filled with relief, but she was also angry that Betty hadn't asked permission to go to her friend's house.

Tip 51: We sometimes say people are **filled with** relief.

100. role /rol/ n.

Meaning: An actor or actress plays a role or a part in a play, a movie, etc. The role he or she plays = the character the actor or actress portrays in the play, movie, etc. Our roles in life = the different relationships and responsibilities we have. We play different roles at different times in our lives. We play different roles with different people. Sometimes we pretend to be something we are not; when we do that, we are also playing a role.

Example:
Right now, I have eight different roles: I am a husband, a father, a son, a teacher, a student, a writer, a computer applications developer and a California Golden Bear basketball fan.

Example:
Robert played the role of a nice guy, but at home he beat his wife.

101. dramatic /drə.mæ.dɪk/ adj.

Other forms: **drama** /dra.mə/ n. **dramatically** /drə.mæ.də.kli/ n.
Opposite: dull
Meaning: Drama refers to the theater and acting: a play is sometimes called a drama. If something is dramatic, it is exciting. If someone does something in an exciting way or obviously in a way an actor or actress might do it, then they are being dramatic.

Example:
She told him dramatically, "If you don't marry me, I'll kill myself." Actually, she was thinking that if they didn't get married, she would move to Istanbul and look for a handsome Turk.

Example:
The end of the movie was pretty dramatic. The cowboy jumped out of the Texas hotel window onto his white horse, grabbed Madonna before she could run away, and rode as fast as his horse would take him away from danger - all the way to Disneyland (where they lived happily ever after).

102. maturation /mæ.chʊr.e.shən/ n.

Other forms: **mature** /mə.chʊr/ adj. **mature** /mə.chʊr/ v.
Opposite (of mature): immature
Meaning: Maturation refers to the process of becoming an adult. Being an adult means acting in a responsible and mature way, i.e. not like a child. Being older doesn't, by itself, make someone mature.

Example:
Can you believe it? Harold is 47 years old and he still acts like an immature teenager. I don't think he'll ever grow up!

Example:
The process of maturation is sometimes a painful one.

Example:
Joy: I'll never speak to him again!
Penny: Why not?
Joy: He didn't pick me up until six. I had to wait a whole 20 minutes!
Penny: Did he have an excuse?
Joy: He said his meeting went too long. I'm through with him!
Penny: C'mon Joy, you can be more mature than that. Call him up and apologize for being angry.

103. spectrum /spɛk.trəm/ n.

Meaning: Spectrum refers to a range or scale. The color spectrum, for example, represents a range of color.

Example:
Her dress was certainly colorful. It had every color of the spectrum in it.

Example:
The political spectrum ranges from radical on the extreme left to reactionary on the extreme right. We could complete the political spectrum in this way: radical (flaming liberal)-liberal-moderate-(middle-of-the-roader)-conservative-reactionary (red-neck)

Example:
Some politicians try to please everybody. Once, President Nixon told his audience, "I am a liberal conservative standing foursquare (right) in the middle of the road." That certainly covers the political spectrum!

104. subtle /sə.dəl/ adj.

Other forms: subtlety /sə.dəl.ti/ n.
Opposite: obvious
Meaning: Something that is subtle is not obvious. It's hard to see something subtle. It may be difficult to understand a subtle remark.

Example:
The subtle colors gave a naturalness to the painting.

Example:
Melissa said, "Frank, I hate you!"
Now, that wasn't very subtle, was it?

105. isolation /ai.so.le.shən/ n.

Other forms: **isolate** /ai.so.let/ v. **isolated** /ai.so.le.dəd/ adj.
Opposite: being with others, included in the group
Meaning: If someone is isolated from others, he or she is separated from them. A person may be physically isolated from others or simply feel isolated from the group.

Example:
The inmate who stabbed his cell mate was put in isolation in a dark cell far away from the rest of the prison population.

Example:
Juan was isolated from the group because he didn't wear baggy pants and a bandanna.

Tip 52: **cell** = room in a jail or prison. If you get **stabbed** with a knife, you bleed, of course.

106. on a single occasion /an ə sɪŋ.gəl.ə.ke.ʒən/ adv.

Other forms: **on one occasion**
Opposite: many times
Meaning: On a single occasion means once, one time.

Example:
Henry is a big fat liar. There hasn't been a single occasion where I have heard him tell the truth.

Example:
I've heard her sing on occasion; unfortunately, there hasn't been a single occasion where she has sung very well.

Tip 53: Don't confuse on a single occasion with **on occasion** which means occasionally.
Tip 54: a big fat liar = a person who lies a lot

107. origin /or.ə.jɪn/ n.

Other forms: **original** /or.ɪ.jə.nəl/ adj.   **originate** /or.ɪ.jə.net/ v.
Opposite: end
Meaning: Where something originates is where it begins. Its origin is its beginning. The original one is the first one.

Example:
My dislike for dogs has its origin in the English Bulldog that bit me in the butt while I was delivering newspapers on Vicente Street in Oakland, California on the morning of July 4th, 1946. I guess he didn't like my independence.

Example:
My hatred for mushroom soup originates from the time I barfed on it when I was five years old.

Tip 55: **Original** is also used to mean **real**, the opposite of **fake**, and **imitation**.
Tip 56: Ten ways to get sick to your stomach (from medical to horrible): **regurgitate, disgorge, retch, vomit, barf, ralph, puke, heave, throw up, upchuck**

108. to coin /koin/ v.

Other forms: **coin** /koin/ n. **coined** /koind/ adj.
Meaning: To coin something means to create it. The government **mints** coins (makes coins). A quarter is a coin. A dime is a coin. A nickel is a coin. A penny is a joke.

Example:
Samuel Clemens coined a pen name for himself from a saying riverboat men used on the Mississippi. What was it? It was Mark Twain.

Example:
Someone, somewhere coined the word barf. Until then, one could only regurgitate, disgorge one's food, retch, vomit, puke, heave, throw up and upchuck.

Example:
Recently coined phrases may or may not last. They may be around for years, they may go out of use and return in a later decade or they may disappear and never be heard from again.

109. evident /ɛ.və.dɛnt/ adj.

Other forms: **evidently** /ɛ.və.dɛnt.li/ adj.
Opposite: hidden
Meaning: When something is evident, everybody can see it. If something is evidently true, it seems to be true. From what we can see, it appears to be true.

Example:
Bob: It was evident from his reaction that he is not going to donate any money for the new library.
Pete: Oh yeah? What'd he say?
Bob: He said he hates to read.

Example:
Evidently, she doesn't like you. (It seems she doesn't like you.) Now take her knife out of your ribs and go home and forget her.

110. transformation /trænz.for.me.shən/ n.

Other forms: **transform** /trænz.form/ v. (-ed/-ing adj)
Opposite (of transformed): unchanged
Meaning: Generally, a transformation is a change from one form to another form. However, a transformation may also represent a change in condition, i.e. the form is the same, but its condition is different.

Example:
The markings made on the female's stomach with the chief's razor-sharp knife represented a transformation from girlhood to womanhood in that African village. As soon as the guys saw the markings, she had to put up with expressions like "Say baby, what's your sign?"

Example:
In his dream, he was transformed into a bird. When he woke up he yawned, stretched his wings, and flew out the window.

This is the brother of the bulldog that chased me.

I don't think she likes me.

Practice 35 : Stress test

Directions : Underline the loudest syllable.

1. infancy 2. condolences 3. ritual 4. funeral 5. transition
6. frightening 7. stressful 8. relieved 9. dramatic
10. maturation 11. spectrum 12. subtle 13. isolation
14. occasion 15. origin 16. evident 17. transformation

Practice 36 : Stickers

Directions : Write a memory sticker from a story or example in the book that will help you remember what each word means. Cross out the words you already know and concentrate on those you don't.

Example: spectrum : color

1. infancy : _____
2. condolences : _____
3. rite : _____
4. ritual : _____
5. funeral : _____
6. transition : _____
7. frightening : _____
8. stressful : _____
9. relieved : _____
10. role : _____
11. dramatic : _____
12. maturation : _____
13. spectrum : _____
14. subtle : _____
15. isolation : _____
16. on a single occasion : _____
17. origin : _____
18. to coin : _____
19. evident : _____
20. transformation : _____

Practice 37 : Using Your Own Experience

Directions : Write your own "story" and memory sticker to help you remember these words. If you already know a word, you don't need a Memory sticker of course, so write stories or examples only for those words you have trouble with.

1. infancy :
   _____

2. condolences :
   _____

3. rites, rituals :
   _____

4. funeral :
   _____

5. transition :
   _____

6. frightening :
   _____

7. stressful :
   _____

8. relieved :
   _____

9. role :
   _____

10. dramatic :
    _____

11. maturation :
    _____

12. spectrum :
    _____

13. subtle :
    _____

14. isolation :
    _____

15. on a single occasion :
_____
_____
16. origin :
_____
_____
17. to coin :
_____
_____
18. evident :
_____
_____
19. transformation :
_____
_____

Practice 38 : Simple Connections

<u>Directions</u> : Choose a word that <u>suggests</u> the meaning of the boldfaced word. Put the appropriate letter in the blank.

a. baby **b.** sorry **c.** change **d.** practices **e.** death **f.** temporary
g. scary **h.** pressure **i.** relaxed **j.** part **k.** exciting **l.** responsible
m. range **n.** subdued **o.** separated **p.** once **q.** beginning
r. create **s.** easy to see

1. Sue was **stressed out** for the entire week her mother-in-law was visiting. __
2. No one caught her **subtle** criticism of the flower arrangements. __
3. The entrance to the new theater is quite **dramatic**. __
4. The frog was **transformed** into a prince. __
5. **Evidently,** you didn't hear me. __
6. As far as we know, infants love **infancy**. __
7. **Maturation** takes time.......but 45 years? __
8. Janice was **relieved** to hear that she wasn't being laid off. __
9. The **transition** from single life to married life isn't always easy. __
10. The night clubs of New Orleans were the **origin** of Jazz. __
11. Alcoholics tend to **isolate** themselves. __
12. ---
     <u>Student</u> : "I *like* totally love it when you *like* read like the Count *like* on Sesame Street."
     <u>Professor</u> : I'd like to murder the person who **coined** the word "like". __
13. Sherry was **frightened** by the large insect in her tea. __
14. The **rites and rituals** in the ceremony evolved over the years. __
15. The **funeral** seemed longer than the honoree's life. __
16. Betty is very **creative**. She used every color in the spectrum in her painting and it still looked good. __
17. Alvin's uncle offered Alvin **condolences** after Alvin and his team lost the Dragon Boat race. __
18. Claudia sang **on a single occasion**. When she was done, the audience laughed so hard they cried. That's why Claudia never sang again. __
19. The President played a **role** in the peace talks, but the final agreement was worked out by his trained negotiators. __

Practice 39 : Similarities

Directions : Write a word in each blank which has a meaning similar to the words given.

1. vomit : _____ _____ _____ _____ _____
2. frighten : _____ _____

Practice 40 : Opposites

Directions : Choose a word that means the opposite of the boldfaced word. Put the appropriate letter in the blank.

a. old age b. permanent c. calm
d. stressed e. dull f. immature g. obvious
h. end i. hidden j. static

1. Mike's job on the firing squad was quite **stressful**, but he certainly wasn't as **stressed** as the people being shot. __
2. Her perfume was **subtle**, but effective. __
3. The chickens made a **dramatic** entry by coming into the banquet room and flying into the salad bowl. __
4. The old ballpark really needs a **transformation**. __
5. It was **evident** from her remarks that she didn't like the Senator. __
6. As far as we know, **infancy** is not very intellectual. __
7. That ghost is very **mature**. It rattles its chains only on holidays. __
8. Jan was **relieved** to hear that her brother in the hospital was OK. __
9. The **transition** from one job to another wasn't easy. __
10. That dance **originated** in Hungary. __

Practice 41 : Do these make sense, or not?

Directions : If the information in the sentence is consistent, if everything fits OK, if there are no contradictions, nothing improbable or impossible, then write YES in the blank. However, if the parts don't fit, if it doesn't make sense, if its ridiculous or absurd, then write NO in the blank.

1. Sue was scared, but she wasn't **frightened** much. __
2. Joe played the **role** of Cleopatra in the play. __
3. Beth's flamenco pink dress with the chartreuse belt and shoes was quite **subtle**. __
4. A librarian has less **stress** on the job than a salesperson. __
5. It's pretty **evident** that money talks. Why doesn't it speak to me? __
6. The movie was so **dramatic** that the audience fell asleep. __
7. The government **coins** money. __
8. **Infants** are orderly. __
9. Maria has our **condolences**. She has three teenagers. __
10. Helen was **relieved** when the mouse left the house. __
11. **Funerals** are a lot of fun. __
12. Ted was extraordinarily tall, so he was obviously **mature**. __
13. They **isolated** the boy by taking him to a football game. __
14. For the old priest, the **rites and rituals** were pretty routine. __
15. Larry **originated** the idea by stealing it from his sister. __

Really?
Directions: Explain your answers to these items :

3. _____
4. _____
5. _____
9. _____

Write
Directions: Write a sentence of your own for each of the words you are learning. Do not write sentences for words you already know. Instead, write a sentence for any substitute words you have chosen to learn.

Lesson 6 Study Guide

Word	Substitute	Similar	Opposite	Memory	✓
infancy					
condolence					
rite					
ritual					
funeral					
transition					
frightening					
stressful					
relieve					
role					
dramatic					
maturation					
spectrum					
subtle					
isolation					
on a single occasion					
origin					
to coin					
evident					
transformation					

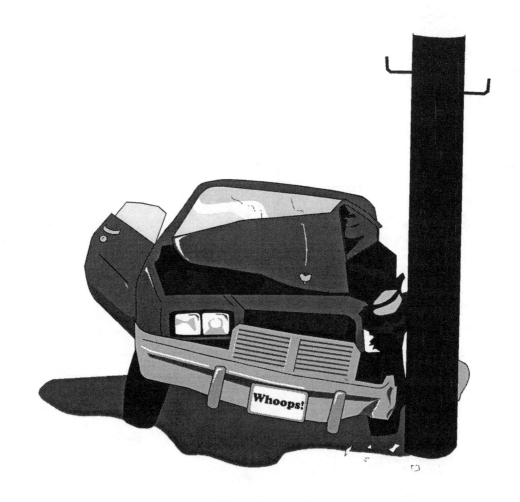

Whoops! Another abrupt turn, another pole.

Lesson 7 Focus Sheet

Word	✓	Subst Word	Listen	Speak	Read	Write
filibuster						
abruptly						
furthermore						
in addition						
moreover						
additionally						
even more						
forbidden						
blissful						
symbolic						
to fast						
deprivation						
yank						
pinch						
ordeal						
humiliated						
sacred						
lifeless						
emergence						
identify with						

Lesson 7

111. filibuster /fɪl.ə.bəs.tər/ n.

Meaning: A filibuster is a special procedure used in the US Senate which allows a Senator or his witnesses to talk for long periods of time in order to prevent a vote from being taken.

Example:
Senator Foghorn got the floor, i.e. he had the right to speak, and he kept it from Friday afternoon until Monday morning. During that time, he talked about southern cooking. He read some of his Mom's recipes and he read recipes from her favorite cookbook. He then asked a number of other southern Senators to read their mothers' recipes and recipes from many other cookbooks. The Senate chambers (room) were filled with the aroma of southern fried chicken when one of the Senators decided to show everyone how to prepare it. On Monday morning, the two Democratic Senators who were absent on Friday arrived. Now the Democrats had enough votes to defeat the Republican bill on welfare reform and Senator Foghorn and his friends stopped talking about southern cooking and called for a vote on the issue. That's a filibuster, folks.

112. abruptly /ə.brəpt.li/ adv.

Other forms: **abrupt** /ə.brəpt/ adj.
Opposite: slowly
Meaning: When something happens abruptly, it happens suddenly or quickly. Abrupt means about the same thing as quick.

Example:
The short man turned abruptly when he saw her out of the corner of his eye and immediately began his introduction by breathing his onion breath all over her new jacket.

Example:
His wife would always give him directions when they were driving somewhere. Alas, she always told him at the last minute where he had to turn, so when she said "Now!" he would make an abrupt turn and crash into a pole or drive up on someone's front porch, or something else of interest. Eventually, they would get to their destination.

Tip 57: quick = /kwɪk/

113. furthermore /fɜr.θər.mor/ adv.
114. in addition /ɪn ə.dɪ.shən/ adv.
115. moreover /mor o.vər/ adv.

116. additionally /ə.dɪ.shən.ə.li/ adv.
117. even more /i.vən mor/ adv.

Meaning: All of the above expressions are transitions (connectors) which mean something like *also*. They tell you that more information about the previous subject is coming.

Example:
Henry's mom, who was very angry at the way he had talked to her, told him to put his bike in the garage and clean his room. Then she added, "Furthermore, after dinner I want you to wash the dishes. And if you ever talk to me that way again, you will wash every window in the house!"
Boy, was she mad!

Example:
In addition to the warnings given earlier, I have one last thing for you to remember: All the treasures of earth cannot bring back one lost moment.

Example:
After the boss complained about the way Rich treated the secretary, she added, "Moreover, if you lose one more client, you can pick up your paycheck!"

Example:
Mr. Burke, the company will offer you a salary of $110,000 per year. Additionally, you will receive medical, dental, vision care, and paid prescription benefits. Even more beneficial in the long run, Mr. Burke, will be our stock option plan under which the company will provide you with five shares of company stock for each share you purchase.

118. forbidden /for.bɪ.dən/ adj.

Other forms: **forbid** /for.bɪd/ v.
Opposite: Sure, it's OK. Go ahead. No problem!
Meaning: If something is forbidden, we are not supposed to have it, see it, do it, etc.
Only someone in authority, someone who has power over us, can forbid us to do something.

Example:
Eve was walking in the garden of Eden one day when she passed a rather attractive snake who was wrapped around the tree of forbidden fruit. As she walked by, he called to her:
Snake: Hey goodlookin', why don't you try some of this great fruit. It'll really open your eyes.
Eve: Oh I couldn't do that. It's forbidden fruit. God told us not to eat any. I distinctly remember Him saying, "Look. Don't touch."
Snake: Yeah, but you know why He doesn't want you to have any of that fruit, don't you?

Eve: Actually, I don't remember Him saying why.
Snake: That's because He didn't. He doesn't want you to know that, if you eat this fruit, you will know as much as God!
Eve: Really?
Snake: You bet. Here............try one.
Eve: Oh, I don't know if I should.
Snake: C'mon. Don't be chicken. It won't kill you.
Eve: Will I really know as much as God?
Snake: Yep. If you eat this stuff for a week. It'll give you a brand new perspective on life.
Eve: Oh Ok. (She takes a huge bite out of the forbidden fruit.)
Snake: Now take some of this fruit to Adam. See if you can get him to try it. Come back to the tree in a week and let me know what you've learned.

A week later......
Eve: Hello? Jake the Snake? Where are you?
Jake: (slithering down a branch of the tree of forbidden fruit) How'd you know my name, Evie?
Eve: God knows your name; therefore....
Jake: Yeah, that makes sense. What else did you learn?
Eve: Well, I learned a lot of things I'd rather not be bothered with. For example, how snails mate. What makes the lead in pencils break when you need to use them the most. Things like that. But I did learn something terrible about Adam.
Jake: What was that?
Eve: Before I knew what God knows, I thought Adam was the greatest guy who ever walked the face of the earth. Now all I see is a guy who watches football games and drinks beer all day and thinks it's OK for women to be paid less for the same job because men are smarter. It's a good thing he's so good with Cain and Able or I'd be out of here.

Example:
Tommy's mom said to him, "I forbid you to play football anymore. You've already broken both legs and now you come home with a broken arm!

119. blissful /blɪs.fʊl/ adj.

Other forms: **bliss** /blɪs/ n. **blissfully** /blɪs.fʊl.li/ adv.
Opposite: unhappiness
Meaning: If you're blissful, you're very happy. You're full of bliss. You look at life blissfully.

Example:
They had been married for not more than a year when one blissful day his wife told him they were going to have a baby.

Example:
Their days were filled with bliss until their baby became a teenager.

120. symbolic /sɪm.bal.ɪk/ adj.

Other forms: **symbol** /sɪm.bəl/ n. **symbolize** /sɪm.bəl.aiz/ v.
Meaning: A symbol is something that represents or "stands for" something else. We can use objects, for example, to represent ideas, e.g. the Statue of Liberty is a symbol of freedom; the symbol /ŋ/ represents the sound usually spelled **ng**, as in sing.

Example:
There is a famous painting of a farmer and his wife. This painting symbolizes the character, attitudes, and lifestyle of the midwest farmer in the first half of the 20th century.

Example:
A heart is symbolic of love. A heart with an arrow through it is....well, you know.

121. to fast /fæst/ v.

Other forms: **fasting** /fæs.tɪg/ n.
Opposite: eat like a pig
Meaning: When someone fasts, he or she stops eating for a relatively long period of time.

Example:
The old man announced to the world that he would not eat again until the government released its political prisoners. He said he would fast until the government changed its policies.

Example:
Moslems fast during Ramadan; Catholics fast during Lent.

Tip 58: **relatively long** = comparatively long = long compared to something else

122. deprivation /dɛ.prə.ve.shən/ n.

Other forms: **deprive** /dɛ.praiv/ v. **deprived** /dɛ.praivd/ adj.
Meaning: If you are deprived of something, either (1) you are not allowed to have something that you have a right to have or (2) something you had is taken away from you.

Example:
When the apartment manager told the Afro-American couple there were no apartments available, when actually there were a number of vacant apartments, he deprived the couple of their right to live anywhere they could afford to live. The couple sued and won. The apartment owners are out a lot of money. The apartment manager is out of a job.

Example:
After Bill saw his sixteen-year-old daughter pull out of the driveway at 40 miles an hour, he took her car keys away and told her she would not be able to drive for a week. In doing so, he deprived her of the right to drive for a week.

Tip 59: **a number of** = several .
Tip 60: **pull out** = **back out** = drive out backwards

123. yank /yæŋk/ v.

Other forms: **yank** /yæŋk/ v.
Opposite (kinda): to be lead gently by the hand
Meaning: Yank means to **pull hard**. You yank something or someone when you grab them and pull them away from their location (from where they are).

Example:
Little Bobby had been crying and yelling in the store for some time. Finally, his mom couldn't take it anymore, so she yanked him by the arm and dragged him kicking and screaming out the door.

Example:
Bobby yanked the toy out of Eben's hand. (You can see that Bobby is really a brat.)

Tip 61: **yell** = shout. **for some time** = for a relatively long time.
brat = a terrible child

124. pinch /pɪnch/ v.

Other forms: **pincher** /pɪnch.ər/ n. **pinchee** /pɪnch.i/ n.
Meaning: Here's the situation: the pincher pinches the pinchee. Get it? How do you pinch someone? Well, you take your thumb and your forefinger (that's the one next to your thumb) and you squeeze them (press them) together with somebody else's skin between them. It hurts (them, not you) like hell.

Example:
Be careful picking up that lobster. It might pinch you.

Example:
My mom never liked to spank us in public. She thought doing that was low class. One day when I was four years old, I was misbehaving in front of the church while my mom was talking to a group of her friends. Smiling at her friends and without interrupting her conversation, she quietly reached out behind her and pinched my arm so hard I thought it would fall off ! I was much better the next time my mom took me to church.

Tip 62: **-er** = the one who does it.   **-ee** = the one who gets it
Tip 63: **spank** = to hit with an open hand, with the palm of the hand.
(**palm** = the inside of a fist. **fist** = a closed hand)

125. ordeal /or.di.əl/ n.

Opposite: easy
Meaning: An ordeal is a difficult **task** (job), a difficult experience, a difficult time.

Example:
Going to the store with my mom was an ordeal (for her).

Example:
Yanking your kid out of the store after listening to 15 minutes of crying and yelling is an ordeal.

Example:
It can be an ordeal for a woman to travel to Italy because pinching foreign women on the butt is a ritual for some men over there.

Tip 64: **butt** = derriere = bum = ass = bottom = behind = backside = can = tail = fanny = keister = rear = rear end = tush

126. humiliated /hyu.mɪl.i.e.dəd/ adj.

Other forms: **humiliate** /hyu.mɪl.i.et/ v. **humiliation** /hyu.mɪl.i.e.shən/ n.
Opposite: praised
Meaning: If you are humiliated, you are very embarrassed by something you did or by something somebody else did that reflects on you (damages your reputation or makes you look stupid).

Example:
Pam felt totally humiliated in front of 500 people in the audience when she stopped in the middle of her speech and couldn't remember what she had planned to say.

Example:
My mom was humiliated by the way I acted in the store, but only temporarily. After promising to behave better next time, I convinced Mom that we should go to Edy's for some ice cream.

127. sacred /se.krəd/ adj.

Other forms: **sacredness** /se.krəd.nəs/ n.
Opposite: denigrated, defamed, not respected
Meaning: Something which is sacred is revered, worthy of respect. Often people use the word sacred to mean holy. In everyday use, sacred is often used to mean "untouchable", "unchangeable".

Example:
Catholics consider the cave at Lourdes to be a sacred place. The black stone in Mecca is a sacred object to Moslems.

Example:
Joe: I think we should make some changes in the proposal.
Bill: Are you kidding? Don't you know who wrote the proposal?
Joe: No I hadn't heard.
Bill: Rose. You know, ROSE - the boss's new wife! Forget trying to change it. It's sacred.

128. lifeless /laif.lɛs/ adj.

Other forms: **life** /laif/ n. **alive** /ə.laiv/ adj.
Opposite : lively
Meaning: A guy who is lifeless may actually be dead, or he simply may not be moving. Sometimes we say a person who doesn't have much energy is lifeless.

Example:
After being shot ten times, the escaped criminal lay lifeless in the pool of blood in the middle of Fifth street.

Example:
He lay on the couch, a lifeless mass, after consuming nine hours of football, three bags of potato chips and twelve beers.

Tip 65: -less = without

129. emergence /i.mər.jəns/ n.

Other forms: **emergent** /i.mər.jənt/ adj. **emerging** /i.mər.jɪŋ/ adj. **emerge** /i.mərj/ v.
Opposite (of emerging): fading
Meaning: To emerge means to appear slowly. It also means growing and expected to continue growing.

Example:
In the middle 1980's, desktop publishing was an emerging technology.

Example:
Their market strategy for distributing the new product emerged from the many meetings they had last month.

Example:
The emergence of so many computer magazines is hard to explain. I don't know how they are going to be able to stay in business.

130. identify with /ə.dɛn.tɪ.fai wɪθ/ adj.

Other forms: **identification** /ə.dɛn.tɪ.fɪ.**ke**.shən/ n.
Opposite: see nothing in common with
Meaning: Someone who identifies with someone else sees something in himself or herself that is like that person. They have something in common, i.e. they share similar values, talents, troubles, and so on.

Example:
Steve identified too much with his brother, who was an ex-con (convict), and later became a drug addict like his brother.

Example:
I have identified most with Martin Luther King.

Tip 66: **and so on** = etc.
Tip 67: **an ex-con** = someone who has been in prison

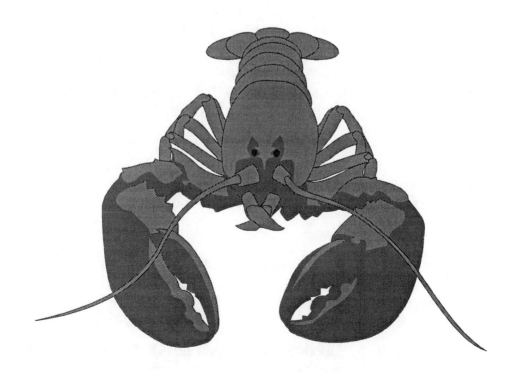

Lobsters pinch.

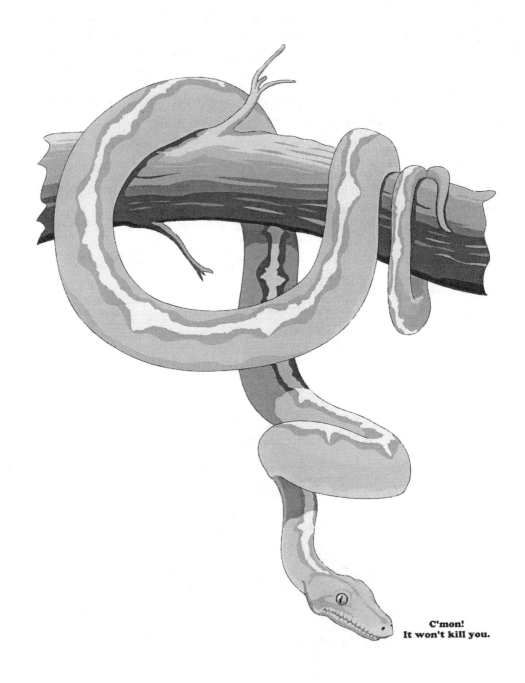

Don't be chicken.

Practice 42 : Stress test

Directions : Underline the loudest syllable.

1. filibuster 2. abruptly 3. furthermore 4. moreover 5. in addition
6. additionally 7. forbidden 8. blissful 9. symbolic
10. deprivation 11. ordeal 12. humiliated 13. sacred
14. lifeless 15. emergence 16. identify with

Practice 43 : Stickers

Directions : Write a memory sticker from a story or example in the book that will help you remember what each word means. Cross out the words you already know and concentrate on those you don't.

Example: forbidden: Eve

1. filibuster : _____
2. abruptly : _____
3. furthermore, moreover, in addition : _____
4. forbidden : _____
5. blissful : _____
6. symbolic : _____
7. to fast : _____
8. deprivation: _____
9. yank : _____
10. pinch : _____
11. ordeal : _____
12. humiliated : _____
13. sacred : _____
14. lifeless : _____
15. emergence : _____
16. identify with : _____

Practice 44 : Using Your Own Experience

Directions : Write your own "story" and sticker to help you remember these words. If you already know a word, you don't need a sticker of course, so write stories or examples only for those words you have trouble with.

1. filibuster :
_____
_____

2. abruptly :
_____
_____

3. furthermore, moreover :
_____
_____

4. forbidden :
_____
_____

5. blissful :
_____
_____

6. symbolic :
_____
_____

7. to fast :
_____
_____

8. deprivation :
_____
_____

9. yank :
_____
_____

10. pinch :
_____
_____

11. ordeal :
_____
_____

12. humiliated :
_____
_____

13. sacred :
_____
_____

14. lifeless :
_____
_____

15. emergence :
_____
_____
16. identify with :
_____
_____

Practice 45 : Simple Connections

Directions : Choose a word that <u>suggests</u> the meaning of the boldfaced word. Put the appropriate letter in the blank.

a. suddenly **b.** also **c.** can't do it **d.** happy **e.** represents **f.** don't eat
g. can't have **h.** pull hard **i.** finger squeeze **j.** difficult **k.** embarrassed
l. holy **m.** dead **n.** grow **o.** something in common

1. Remodeling the studio was an **ordeal**. The wrong materials were delivered; the city lost the permits; the workers didn't show up until a week after we were supposed to start. And that was only the beginning of our troubles. __
2. Feeding the giants is **forbidden**. __
3. Sue was enthusiastically **pinched** in Rome, Naples and Venice. __
4. The naturalist received an **abrupt** welcome to the forest by the huge bear. __
5. He was **humiliated** when the bear chased him up a tree. __
6. **Moreover**, he was further humiliated when the bear left her little bear cubs to guard him. __
7. A **filibuster** is one of the few ways one can waste time to get an advantage. __
8. Rose spent a **blissful** afternoon painting in her studio. __
9. Unexpectedly, genius **emerged** from the shy but curious boarding school girl. __
10. You can't **deprive** anyone of their potential, but you can take away their opportunity. __
11. Jack sat there **lifelessly** until he jumped to conclusions. __
12. The turtle is **symbolic** of long life, i.e. it is a **symbol** of longevity. __
13. **In addition**, the turtle pees pure water. __
14. **Furthermore**, turtles make great soup. __
15. Unfortunately, I'm **fasting**. __
16. I can't **identify with** temperamental people because I'm so even tempered. __
17. His aunt **yanked** Billy into the studio by the arm and sat him down at the piano to practice. __
18. Cows are **sacred** in India. Money is **sacred** on Wall Street. __

Practice 46 : Similarities

<u>Directions</u>: Write a word in each blank which has a meaning similar to the words given.

1. in addition : _____ _____ _____ _____
2. ass : _____ _____ _____ _____ _____

Practice 47 : Opposites

<u>Directions</u>: Choose a word that means the opposite of the boldfaced word. Put the appropriate letter in the blank.

a. slowly **b.** Sure, go ahead. **c.** sad
d. lead gently by the hand **e.** It's yours. **f.** easy **g.** praised
h. eat a lot **i.** fade **j.** nothing in common

1. Unfamiliar insects **emerged** from the kitchen cabinet like soldiers marching into battle. __
2. Her perfume **yanked** him by the nose and threw him to the ground. __
3. The unsuspecting turkey lived a **blissful** life in the beautiful garden until Thanksgiving day. __
4. Moreover, it was **deprived of** a funeral. __
5. Becoming mature is really an **ordeal** for Rose Anne. __
6. Going from infancy to old age seemed uncommonly **abrupt** to the 90-year-old man. __
7. Transforming the turtle into turtle soup would have been an excellent idea if she had not been **fasting**. __
8. Feeding the fish was **forbidden**. __
9. The audience was sympathetic with the singer, for they could see that she was **humiliated** by forgetting the words to the song. __
10. His dog **identified with** George. The dog felt that he and George had similar appetites, similar roles and similar intelligence. __

Practice 48: Do these make sense, or not?

Directions: If the information in the sentence is consistent, if everything fits OK, if there are no contradictions, nothing improbable or impossible, then write YES in the blank. However, if the parts don't fit, if it doesn't make sense, if its ridiculous or absurd, then write NO in the blank.

1. The professor was **humiliated** during his class when a student told him that his fly was open. ___
2. Ben left the room **abruptly**. Later on, we found out that he had to go to the bathroom. ___
3. Paula **pinched** Peter to wake him up before the teacher got to his desk. ___
4. **Fasting**, of course, refers to speed. ___
5. The **ordeal** was easily accomplished in just a few minutes. ___
6. The Senator is so old that he doesn't buy green bananas anymore, and he certainly doesn't lead any filibusters. ___
7. "**Deprivation** isn't always a bad thing," Sam said, as they took away the garbage. ___
8. Breathing during my lecture is **forbidden**. ___
9. The **lifeless** chicken was dead. ___
10. Carl was filled with **bliss** when the cab left without him. ___
11. Alex **emerged** from the dental office with a toothless smile. ___
12. Ted was brainless, so - naturally - the genius could **identify with** him. ___
13. The coach **yanked** Gary gently off the field after he was injured. ___
14. For the old priest, the cross was a **symbol** of security. ___
15. His word is **sacred**. He will lie only for money. ___

Really?
Directions: Explain your answers to these items :

5. _____
6. _____
7. _____
8. _____
10. _____
13. _____
15. _____

Write
Directions: Write a sentence of your own for each of the words you are learning. Do not write sentences for words you already know. Instead, write a sentence for any substitute words you have chosen to learn.

Lesson 7 Study Guide

Word	Substitute	Similar	Opposite	Memory	✓
filibuster					
abruptly					
furthermore					
in addition					
moreover					
additionally					
even more					
forbidden					
blissful					
symbolic					
to fast					
deprivation					
yank					
pinch					
ordeal					
humiliated					
sacred					
lifeless					
emergence					
identify with					

Cyclops had tunnel vision.

Lesson 8 Focus Sheet

Word	✓	Subst Word	Listen	Speak	Read	Write
productive						
solidarity						
renew						
incorporation						
healed						
status						
feast						
mask						
reveal						
relearn						
conclude						
foreign						
razor						
navel						
vertical						
horizontal						
diagonal						
charcoal						
infected						
bathe						

Lesson 8

131. productive /prə.dək.tɪv/ adj.

Other forms: **produce** /prə.dus/ v. **production** /prə.dək.shən/ n.
Opposite: not much done
Meaning: A productive person gets a lot done, accomplishes a lot. A productive idea or plan has positive results.

Example:
The change in HR procedures had productive results. For example, employees were able to get vacations when they wanted them, the company had better sick leave records, and employee complaints were processed more quickly.

Example:
Apple's production wasn't able to keep up with demand, so many orders were not filled even four months after they were placed.

Tip 68: **HR** = the Human Resources Office of a company (In some companies, it is still called the Personnel Office.)
Tip 69: **demand** = what consumers were willing to buy

132. solidarity /sal.lə.dɛr.ə.ti/ n.

Other forms: **solid** /sa.ləd/ n. **solidify** /sə.lɪ.dɪ.fai/ v. (-ly adv)
Opposite: disunity
Meaning: A group's solidarity refers to its unity or togetherness. When there is solidarity among members of the group, they are willing to stick together even - or especially - in the face of trouble.

Example:
When the company reduced employee salaries without notice, it solidified the union. They had not been that united in years.

Example:
The union members were solidly behind the union leaders after that.

Tip 70: **stick together** = remain united

133. renew /ri.nu/ v.

Other forms: **renewal** /ri.nu.əl/ n. **renewal** /ri.nud/ adj.
Opposite: weaken
Meaning: When something has become weak, but then becomes stronger again, it is renewed or restored.

Example:
Moving to the hot, dry climate of Arizona renewed Leroy's health. After the move, he no longer suffered much from arthritis.

Example:
After eating that huge piece of strawberry cheesecake, Sam renewed his intention to lose weight.

134. incorporation /ɪn.kor.pər.e.shən/ n.

Other forms: **incorporate** /ɪn.kor.pər.et/ v. **incorporated** /ɪn.kor.pər.e.dəd/ adj.
Opposite: exclude
Meaning: To incorporate means to include. Incorporation refers to the process of inclusion.

Example:
Incorporation rites are designed to show that the youth is now included in the adult group.

Example:
The corporate lawyers incorporated those provisions into the contract with the suppliers to protect the company against having to pay for defective parts.

Tip 71: **provisions of a contract** = parts of an agreement
Tip 72: **defective** = has flaws or defects = doesn't work properly

135. healed /hi.əld/ adj.

Other forms: **heal** /hi.əl/ v.
Opposite: injure, damage, make worse
Meaning: When a very sick person becomes well again, we say that person is healed, i.e. the person isn't ill anymore; he or she is cured.

Example:
The medicine Janet was taking was supposed to heal her, but it almost killed her.

Example:
After the cuts on the girl's stomach healed, scars remained, showing everyone in the village that she was now a woman.

Tip 73: **scar** = marks left after a deep cut has healed

136. status /stæ.dəs/ n.

Meaning: People judge other people and they place them in categories according to various criteria. One's status, or level (how high one is placed) is determined by such things as how rich one is, how educated one is, one's job title or position. It may even be determined by how many children or wives or cattle (cows) one has. Status is also used to inquire about the condition of things and the completeness of processes.

Example:
Harry: Hey Helen, what's the status of that report?
Helen: It was about half done this morning, so they should be finished with it sometime tomorrow afternoon.

Example:
Her status in the company improved greatly after she married the boss's son.

Example:
Before, no one would listen to him even though he had some pretty good ideas. However, his status has been greatly improved since he won $50 million in the lottery - and they now listen to what he says.

Example:
General Powell has a considerably higher status than Private Green.

Tip 74: **greatly** = very much   **considerably** = very much

137. feast /fist/ v.

Other forms: **feast** /fist/ n.
Opposite: starve
Meaning: A feast is a huge meal with many different kinds of fancy, gourmet dishes. The verb *to feast* means to enjoy eating all that stuff (until later when you weigh yourself on the bathroom scale).

Example:
There was a huge feast in the village after the puberty rites were completed.

Example:
They feasted on pheasant, lobster, the best sea bass, and filet mignon - not to mention the caviar, and to say nothing of the wonderful garlic sauce for the escargot, or the Dom Peringion champagne.

Tip 75: **gourmet food** = fancy, well-prepared, delicious food
Tip 76: **not to mention** = in addition to, as well as, besides
Tip 77: **to say nothing of** = let alone = not to mention

138. mask /mæsk/ n.

Other forms: **mask** /mæsk/ v.
Opposite: the real thing
Meaning: People wear masks when they don't want others to know who they are. To mask means to hide what is real.

Example:
Children wear costumes and masks on Halloween when they dress up as scary witches and devils and monsters like Frankenstein.

Example:
The bank robbers wore masks so they couldn't be identified.

Example:
Her smile masked her feelings. He didn't know it, but she was so bored with him she could hardly keep awake.

Example:
Stranger: Say, that's a great witch's mask you're wearing.
Lynn: I'm not wearing a mask!

139. reveal /ri.vi.əl/ v.

Other forms: **revelation** /rɛ.və.**le**.shən/ n.
Opposite: hide
Meaning: To reveal means to show, so a revelation is what has been shown, of course.

Example:
It was quite a revelation when she found out that her boyfriend was married.

Example:
The investigation revealed that the company had been dumping toxic wastes into the river.

Tip 78: **toxic wastes** = poisonous garbage

140. relearn /ri.lərn/ v.

Other forms: **relearning** /ri.lərn.ɪn/ n.
Opposite: unlearn
Meaning: To relearn means to learn again, learn over again.

Example:
After the accident, it was very difficult for him. He had to relearn many things. For example, he had to learn how to walk again.

Example:
I had taken German in high school, but I had to relearn it when I went to Germany twenty years later. I'll tell ya, a lot of relearning took place in the Zum Schwann gasthaus.

Tip 79: **learn over again** = to learn something again after forgetting it

141. conclude /kən.klud/ v.

Other forms: **conclusion** /kən.klu.ʒən/ n. **conclusive** /kən.klu.sɪv/ adj.
Opposite: inconclusive
Meaning: Conclusion means something like the final result. It can be the result of a thinking process or the result of some activity. Conclusive means convincing, i.e. there is enough evidence or enough facts to prove that its true.

Example:
There was conclusive evidence that Jimmie had eaten the cookies. There were cookie crumbs all over his face and on his sweatshirt.

Example:
After twenty minutes of discussion about where they were going to go for dinner, the conclusion was Angelino's pizza.

Example:
The HR Director concluded that Jonathan would not be a good salesman because he wasn't aggressive enough, so she didn't hire him.

Tip 80: **aggressive** = assertive = energetic and outgoing
Tip 81: **energetic** = having lots of energy
Tip 82: We **reach** or **arrive at** conclusions.

142. foreign /for.ən/ adj.

Other forms: **foreigner** /for.ən.ər/ n.
Opposite: familiar
Meaning: Something that is foreign to us is strange or unfamiliar. We are not used to it; we not comfortable with it; we don't understand it very well.

Example:
At first, George had a tough time at his new job as a programmer. He knew Cobalt and FORTRAN and Basic, but C++ was completely foreign to him. However, he learned it pretty quickly, and now he's OK.

Example:
Those conservative corporate investors like foreign investment and foreign labor, but they don't like foreigners.

Tip 83: **tough time** = difficult time = hard time

143. razor /re.zər n.

Other forms: **razor** /re.zər/ adj.
Meaning: In the US and elsewhere guys shave their faces with razors and gals shave their legs and their armpits with razors. Razors contain razor blades which are very thin and very sharp. Cutting someone with a razor produces a thin cut. Razor-sharp means very, very sharp.

Example:
The chief made the marks on her stomach with a razor-sharp knife.

Example:
The razor-sharp claws of the tiger sunk into the cow's back.

Tip 84: **elsewhere** = in other places

144. navel /ne.vəl/ adj.

Meaning: Your navel is your belly button, that strange-looking thing in the middle of your stomach.

Example:
The chief cut a circle with the razor around her navel.

Example:
Speaking of navels and belly buttons, do you have an innie or an outie? (Does your navel go in or stick out of your belly?)

Tip 85: Don't confuse **navel** with **naval**. Naval refers to **the Navy**. You know, sailors and ships and the sea and things like that.
Tip 86: **stick out** = protrude

145. vertical /vər.də.kəl/ adj.
146. horizontal /hor.ɪ.zan.təl/ adj
147. diagonal /dai.æ.gən.əl/ adj

Meaning: Vertical means straight up. Horizontal means straight across. Diagonal means from corner to corner. Got it?

Example:
Larry painted a red horizontal line on each side of his car, from the front of the car to the back.

Example:
The flag pole was a vertical marker for the administration building.

Example:
Professor Cunningham got the idea that Jane didn't like one of the comments he had made on her paper. Jane had drawn two diagonal lines in the form of an X through it.

148. charcoal /char.kol/ n.

Meaning: The black substance that is left after wood has been burned.

Example:
The chief placed charcoal inside the cuts he had made with the razor, so the cuts would get infected and leave a scar after the infection had healed. No infection, no scar. No scar, no transformation.

Tip 87: **burnt** = burned (by fire)

149. infected /ɪn.fɛk.təd/ adj.

Other forms: **infection** /ɪn.fɛk.shən/ n. **infect** /ɪn.fɛkt/ v.
infectious /ɪn.fɛk.shəs/ adj.
Opposite: cure
Meaning: People become infected with disease from bacteria and viruses, but we don't normally say "I am infected with the flu." We say "I have the flu." or "I've got the flu." or "Hey man, stay away from me. You got the flu, man!" If a disease is infectious, it is communicable, i.e. other people can get it from you if you've got it.

Example:
Every winter, I seem to get an ear infection, so I take antibiotics, which gets rid of the infection (until next winter).

Example:
TB is a very infectious disease. So is polio. So is love.

150. bathe /beð/ v.

Other forms: **bath** /bæθ/ n. **bathroom** /bæθ.rum/ n.
Opposite: remain dirty
Meaning: When we bathe, we take a bath, which gets us clean. Normally, we do that in a bath tub or a shower, which can be found in the bathroom. But we can also bathe in a river if a bathroom isn't around. *Bathe* is a very formal word; we don't normally say, "I bathed today." We say, "I took a bath today." Actually, we normally don't tell people whether we've taken a bath or not. How would you like it if somebody asked, "Did you take a bath today?"

Example:
The guards all turned their backs as the princess bathed in the river. It was very hard, but none of the guards looked.

Example:
George slipped on a bar of soap in the bath tub and fell out of the tub onto the bathroom floor, injuring his pride and breaking his nose.

Tip 88: **normally** = usually

A slob is not dignified.

Practice 49 : Stress test

Directions : Underline the loudest syllable.

1. productive 2. solidarity 3. renew 4. incorporation
5. status 6. conclude 7. reveal 8. relearn 9. razor
10. foreign 11. navel 12. vertical 13. horizontal
14. diagonal 15. charcoal 16. infected

Practice 50 : Stickers

Directions : Write a sticker from a story or example in the book that will help you remember what each word means. Cross out the words you already know and concentrate on those you don't.

Example: status : <u>General Powell</u>

1. productive : _____
2. solidarity : _____
3. renew : _____
4. incorporation : _____
5. healed: _____
6. status : _____
7. feast : _____
8. mask: _____
9. reveal : _____
10. relearn: _____
11. conclude : _____
12. foreign : _____
13. razor: _____
14. navel : _____
15. vertical : _____
16. horizontal : _____
17. diagonal : _____
18. charcoal: _____
19. infected : _____
20. bathe : _____

Practice 51 : Using Your Own Experience

Directions : Write your own "story" and memory label to help you remember these words. If you already know a word, you don't need a sticker, of course, so write stories or examples only for those words you have trouble with.

1. productive :

2. solidarity :

3. renew :

4. incorporate :

5. healed :

6. status :

7. feast :

8. mask :

9. reveal :

10. relearn :

11. conclude :

12. foreign :

13. razor :

14. navel :

15. vertical : _____
_____

16. horizontal : _____
_____

17. diagonal : _____
_____

18. charcoal : _____
_____

19. infected : _____
_____

20. bathe : _____
_____

Practice 52 : Simple Connections

Directions : Choose a word that <u>suggests</u> the meaning of the boldfaced word. Put the appropriate letter in the blank.

a. accomplish **b.** unity **c.** strengthen **d.** include **e.** cure **f.** position
g. devour **h.** hide **i.** show **j.** learn again **k.** finish
l. unfamiliar **m.** sharp **n.** belly button **o.** up **p.** across **q.** angle **r.** burned
s. communicable **t.** take a bath

1. There was no **solidarity** among the workers after the boss said he was laying off 40% of the work force. __
2. After the fast, they **feasted** . __
3. After we discovered that Mike, his secretary Charlene, $2 million and a book about Bermuda were missing, we **concluded** that Mike had gone to Bermuda with the secretary. __
4. Ted thought he had put his **razor** in the car, but he hadn't, so he had to go into the important meeting unshaven. __
5. **Bathe** in the sunlight while you can. Your kids come home from school in 17 minutes. __
6. The Grand Jury report **revealed** that two judges had been taking money from defendants whose cases they were hearing. __
7. When Phil had almost finished, he noticed a **foreign** object in his rice. When he looked more closely, he was horrified to see that it was somebody's badly decayed tooth. (true story) __
8. Dave **renewed** his subscription to <u>NewMedia</u> magazine. __
9. Sam hadn't played for a long time, so he had to **relearn** how to play ma-jong. __
10. The lawyers **incorporated** two provisions into the contract with the suppliers: (1) The suppliers would replace all defective parts.
(2) The suppliers would pay shipping costs for all returned defective parts and replacement parts. __---
11. It always took Clarence 20 minutes to get **vertical** in the morning. __
12. The company claimed that its product could heal all **infections**. __
13. The chief put **charcoal** in the cuts he had made on her stomach. __
14. Your **navel** is the point at which you were connected to your mother. __
15. When the boss offered the workers a bonus, they became more **productive**. __
16. An executive has a high **status** and a manual laborer has a low status, even though the manual laborer may be a kind and generous person and the executive a jerk. __
17. ---
    <u>Sarah:</u> You'd better put your **mask** on now.
    <u>Cindy</u>: I'm already wearing it.
    <u>Sarah</u> (icily): Oh... sorry. I couldn't tell. __
18. Mike was **horizontal** after the all-night party. __
19. Pam shouted about 14 terrible expressions and dug a **diagonal** line through her poem. __

Practice 53 : Similarities

Directions : Write a word in each blank which has a meaning similar to the words given.

1. in addition : _____ _____ _____ _____
2. ass : _____ _____ _____ _____ _____

Practice 54 : Opposites

Directions : Choose a word that means the opposite of the boldfaced word. Put the appropriate letter in the blank.

a. disunity b. weaken c. exclude d. starve e. hide f. unlearn g. start
h. familiar i. dull j. stink

1. There was **solidarity** in the office after the supervisor humiliated the bookkeeper. __
2. On Chinese New Year, they **feasted** on roast suckling pig, shark fin soup, Mandarin Duck, and lots of other goodies. __
3. The accounting department **concluded** the ordeal by providing the client with 450 pages of data, and then they went to Angelino's for pizza. __
4. He was so nervous about the job interview that he cut himself three times with his **razor** while he was shaving. __
5. **Bathe** once a day and you can throw the deodorant away. __
6. Sally **revealed** how she really felt about Buddy by paying for his funeral. The only problem was that Buddy was still alive. __
7. Harry noticed a **foreign** object on his desk. It was someone else's nameplate. __
8. Don **renewed** his intention to pay his bills on time, for the 78th time. __
9. Sam decided that he had to **relearn** how to play poker after he lost $1,000 to his mother-in-law. __
10. The publisher **incorporated** two provisions into the contract that the writer didn't like. __

Practice 55: Do these make sense, or not?

Directions: If the information in the sentence is consistent, if everything fits OK, if there are no contradictions, nothing improbable or impossible, then write YES in the blank. However, if the parts don't fit, if it doesn't make sense, if its ridiculous or absurd, then write NO in the blank.

1. Their **solidarity** was **solid** but they were not united. __
2. In another argument with his Mom, Will **renewed** his threat to join the military. __
3. After severe damage to her hand in the accident, Paula sat in her studio attempting to **relearn** how to paint. __
4. The CEO **concluded** the meeting by giving his opening remarks. __
5. The **mask** revealed his identity. __
6. Larry didn't take care of the cut on his hand and it got **infected**. __
7. The boss wouldn't give the workers a raise, so they became more **productive**. __
8. **Feasts** are forbidden during Ramadon. __
9. George injured his belly button, but his **navel** was OK. __
10. It's a good idea to **bathe** before a date. __
11. A flag pole is **vertical**. __
12. The dead man was **horizontal**. __
13. Carl **healed** Sam's black eye by hitting him again - *hard* - in that eye. __
14. It was **foreign** for the introvert to be giving a speech to 500 people. __
15. Gary **incorporated** the boss's suggestions into the report, so the boss fired him. __
16. The professor had high **status**, but no money. __
17. His basic generosity was **revealed** when the rich man gave his daughter a pillow for her wedding gift. __

Really?
Directions: Explain your answers to these items:

1. _____
5. _____
7. _____
10. _____
16. _____

Write
Directions: Write a sentence of your own for each of the words you are learning. Do not write sentences for words you already know. Instead, write a sentence for any substitute words you have chosen to learn.

Lesson 8 Study Guide

Word	Substitute	Similar	Opposite	Memory	✓
productive					
solidarity					
renew					
incorporation					
healed					
status					
feast					
mask					
reveal					
relearn					
conclude					
foreign					
razor					
navel					
vertical					
horizontal					
diagonal					
charcoal					
infected					
bathe					

Venus is the goddess of love.

Lesson 9 Focus Sheet

Word	✓	Subst Word	Listen	Speak	Read	Write
corn husk						
mythical						
goddess						
massage						
vigorous						
similarity						
fictitious						
reinforce						
hardship						
dignity						
rejection						
X accounts for Y						
impress upon						
harsh						
oppressive						
vitality						
judgment						
primary						
threaten						

Lesson 9

151. corn husk /kɔrn həsk/ n.

Other forms: **an ear of corn** /ə.nir.əv.kɔrn/ n. **corn on the cob** /kɔrn an ðə kab/ n. **a kernal of corn** /ə kər. nəl əv kɔrn/ n. **a corn cob** /ə kɔrn kab/ n.
Meaning: We call corn out in the corn field *ears of corn* because they look like ears sticking out on each side of the corn stalk. However, if you cook them and put them on somebody's plate for dinner, they are called *corn on the cob*. When you have eaten all the kernals of corn off the cob, all you have left is the cob. The cob is what you find on the inside; the corn husk is what is on the outside. The husk protects the corn from the weather and the insects in the corn field.

Example:
The home-made tamales (a Mexican dish that is *muy delicioso*) were wrapped in corn husks. I would die for one of them right now.

Example:
Safeway had corn on sale: five ears for a dollar.

152. mythical /mɪ.θə.kəl/ adj.

Other forms: **myth** /mɪθ/ n.
Opposite: real
Meaning: A myth is a story or tale from the distant past which most people assume are not true. Mythical figures (people) or creatures, according to most folks, never existed, except in stories. We often call stories or reports that are not true myths.

Example:
Cyclops, the one-eyed giant, is one example of a mythical creature from Greek mythology.

Example:
Mary: I heard that Apple Computer is going out of business.
Jane: No Mary, that's a myth. We hear something like that every year, but there's no truth to it.

Tip 89: **distant past** = thousands of years ago, before recorded history (before history was written down)

153. Goddess /ga.dəs/ n.

Other forms: **God** /gad/ n. **God-like** /gad laik/ adj.
Meaning: A goddess is a female god.

Example:
It's difficult to live with the god-like qualities I have, especially my humility, but I try.

Example:
In Roman mythology, Venus was the goddess of love.

154. massage /mə.saj/ v.

Other forms: **massage** /mə.saj/ n. **massage parlor** /mə.saj par.lər/ n.
Opposite: Beat somebody up.
Meaning: You can go to a massage parlor to get a massage. At the parlor, the masseuse massages your body for a price. The masseuse puts oil on your body and rubs, pats, and hits it to help you relax.

Example:
The police put the massage parlor out of business because the masseuses were offering more than massages.

155. vigorous /vɪg.ər.əs/ adj.

Other forms: **invigorated** /ɛn.vɪg.ər.e.dəd/ adj. **vigor** /vɪg.ər/ n.
Opposite: slow and lifeless
Meaning: A vigorous person is energetic. He or she has lots of energy. When we feel invigorated, we feel we have lots of energy; we feel more "alive".

Example:
Vigorous work requires lots of energy.

Example:
The cold of the early morning invigorated the old man. On that morning, he felt he could live forever.

156. similarity /sɪm.əl.ɛr.ə.di/ n.

Other forms: **similar** /sɪm.ə.lər/ adj.
Opposite: dissimilar
Meaning: When two or more people, objects, etc. are similar, they are alike in some way; they are like each other in some way; they have similarities.

Example:
Luke and his brother Matthew are similar in that they are both tall and skinny, but they are certainly not similar in appearance in all respects. Luke has blond hair and Matthew has black hair. Luke has blue eyes and Matt has brown eyes. Actually, Matt has one black and blue eye because somebody elbowed him in a basketball game yesterday.

Example:
The Republican and Democratic plans for cutting the budget were similar in some respects; they both called for a reduction in spending, for example. They were dissimilar in that the Republican plan called for deep cuts in health care spending while the Democratic plan called for much smaller cuts in those programs.

Tip 90: **in all respects** = in every way
Tip 91: **skinny** = very thin
Tip 92: **blond** = yellowish (-ish = like, similar to)
Tip 93: **to elbow** = hit someone with an elbow
Tip 94: **in that** = in the respect that = in the sense that

157. fictitious /fɪk.tɪ.shəs/ adj.

Other forms: **fictitious** /fɪk.shən/ n.
Opposite: true
Meaning: Fictitious means false, not real.

Example:
When the escaped convict registered at the hotel, he didn't use his real name; he used a fictitious name.

Example:
If you start your own company and you want to do business under a name that is not your own, you have to file a fictitious name statement with the county.

158. reinforce /ri.ən.fors/ v.

Other forms: **reinforcement** /ri.ən.fors.mənt/ n.
Opposite: weaken
Meaning: You reinforce something when you stress it or emphasize it in some way. When you reinforce something, you make it stronger. Sometimes, people use reinforce to mean emphasize again.

Example:
Sandy reinforced her view that the garbage company was charging too much for services by including comprehensive data in her report on garbage company charges and expenses.

Example:
In its newspaper ad, K-Mart reinforced sale items by printing them in large, boldface type.

Tip 95: comprehensive data = complete information
Tip 96: **This is boldface type.** This is plain type. *This is italic type.*

159. hardship /hard.shɪp/ n.

Other forms: **hard** /hard/ adj.
Opposite: easy, no problem, piece of cake
Meaning: If something is hard, it is difficult, of course. A hardship is an experience or a condition that is difficult.

Example:
Working full time and going to school full time was a hardship for Susan, but she was finally able to get her degree after eight years of studying and working.

Example:
Raising five children without a husband was a hardship for Theresa.

160. dignity /dɪg.nə.ti/ n.

Other forms: **dignify** /dɪg.nə.fai/ v. **dignified** /dɪg.nə.faid/ adj.
Opposite: no class
Meaning: Dignity refers to one's self-respect, the sense that you have value, that you are to be respected because you are you. To act in a dignified way means to act in a way that is both proper and worthy of you. If you dignify something, you give it dignity when it does not have it.

Example:
There's a story about St. Lawrence who was martyred (killed) because he was a Christian. The story tells how he died with great dignity. He was tied to a log (wood from a tree) which was placed on two supports over a fire and he was roasted to death. Before he died, he said to his executioners, "Turn me over. I'm done on this side."

Example:
On Saturdays, George is usually a slob: he doesn't shave, his clothes are wrinkled and his hair is uncombed. However, on Sundays in church he looks very dignified: he is clean shaven, his suit is neatly pressed, and his hair is combed. He looks like a gentleman.

Example:
Don't dignify that question with an answer. (The question is not worthy of an answer; it doesn't deserve an answer; the question is impolite or improper.)

161. rejection /ri.jɛk.shən/ n.

Other forms: **reject** /ri.jɛkt/ v. **rejected** /ri.jɛk.təd/ adj.
Opposite: acceptance
Meaning: Someone who is rejected is not accepted by another person or a group. If that's the case, the rejected person has to deal with being rejected. Rejection is not easy to take; it's not easy to accept.

Example:
Dana, who was eight years old, felt rejected when no one would take her comments seriously.

Example:
After years of rejection, Fred left his wife for Marion, the librarian.

162. X accounts for Y /ə.kauns for/ Idiom

Opposite: unexplainable
Meaning: This accounts for that = this **explains** that. To account for something also means to explain what happened to it.

Example:
Baby Louie started to cry, so his mom gave him a bottle. Instead of drinking it, Louie continued to cry, so his mom checked his diapers and discovered that Louie had pooped in his pants. The dirty diapers accounted for Baby Louie's unhappiness.

Example:
When the lawyer asked him where he was the night of the murder, he couldn't account for his whereabouts.

Tip 97: **pooped** = went number two (in a very different context, **pooped** means very tired)
Tip 98: **his whereabouts** = where he was

163. impress upon /ɪm.prɛs ə.pan/ v.

Meaning: When something is impressed upon you, you are shown how important it is.

Example:
When his computer crashed and he lost a whole day's work on his book, it was impressed upon him that he had better save his work often. Losing a whole day's work impressed upon him the importance of saving his work often.

Example:
When Dick, who was ten years old, returned the wallet he had found, the owner gave him $100. That impressed upon him the value of being honest.

Tip 99: **His computer crashed.** = his computer died = it stopped working and had to be restarted

164. harsh /harsh/ adj.

Other forms: **harshly** /harsh.li/ adv. **harshness** /harsh.nəs/ n.
Opposite: gentle
Meaning: When someone acts in a harsh way, he or she is being nasty, severe, unkind, discourteous. When conditions are harsh, they are very bad.

Example:
When his mom yelled at him, you would think he had robbed a bank or something. All he did was leave his books on the table, and his mom told him he was lazy and inconsiderate. She was very tired from working all day and she had had a very bad day, but her words were much too harsh for the situation.

Example:
Heather couldn't get to the theater from Brooklyn because of the harsh weather; it had been snowing for days and no one could get into Manhattan.

165. oppressive /o.prɛ.sɪv/ adj.

Other forms: **oppression** /o.prɛ.shən/ n. **oppress** /o.prɛs/ v.
Opposite: treated well
Meaning: People who are oppressed are treated in an unfair way by someone who has power over them. They may also be controlled by their oppressors.

Example:
Black slaves were oppressed by the white plantation owners in the South before the Civil War in the United States.

Example:
Immigrant garment workers have been oppressed by some clothing manufacturers, who make them work long hours, sewing fourteen hours a day for very litle pay.

166. vitality /vai.tæl.ə.ti/ n.

Other forms: **vital** /vai.təl/ adj.
Opposite: lacking energy
Meaning: *La dolce vita*, in Italian, means the sweet life. Someone who has a lot of vitality has a lot of energy, a lot of "life". Vital, on the other hand, means very, very important.

Example:
Heather, my oldest daughter, has a lot of vitality. She does eight shows a week in "Grease" on Broadway. She runs around town doing radio commercials and auditioning for other parts. At the same time, she's busy fixing up her apartment in Brooklyn.

Example:
Madonna and Michael Jackson have a lot of vitality on stage.

Tip 100: **on the other hand** = however

167. judgement /jəj.mənt/ n.

Other forms: **judge** /jəj/ v.
Meaning: Judgement = the conclusions drawn (made) by someone after considering the facts.

Example:
Because we cannot see the long-term results of today's actions, we must wait for the judgement of history to determine whether Bill Clinton was a good President or not.

Example:
Who can judge whether General Powell could have been elected the first Black-American President of the United States?

168. primary /prai.mɛr.i/ adj.

Other forms: **prime** /praim/ adj.
Opposite: last, least important
Meaning: Primary and prime mean the first or most important or best event, idea, etc.

Example:
The primary reason, the principle reason, the chief reason, she didn't marry him was, to put it in her words, "He has ugly feet."

Example:
Prime time TV commercials are much more expensive than commercials run during hours when fewer people are watching.

Example:
The CEO gave Harold's report prime consideration because he has a great deal of respect for Harold's wisdom and long experience. Unfortunately, Harold's department head is laying off Harold at the end of the month because Harold is "too old".

Tip 101: **a great deal of** = a lot of
Tip 102: **wisdom** = knowledge from experience

169. threaten /θrɛt.ən/ v.

Other forms: **threat** /θrɛt/ n. **threatening** /θrɛt.nɪŋ/ adj.
Opposite: make someone feel safe and comfortable
Meaning: If you threaten people, you tell them that you will harm them, hurt them in some way.
Example:
Tommy threatened to tell Billy's mom that it was Billy who broke the window if Billy didn't let him ride his new bicycle.

Example:
While she was stopped at the stoplight, Marcie was threatened by a teenage gang member, who waved a large hunting knife in her face. He laughed when he saw the frightened look on her face as she drove away. It's a good thing that Marcie always locks her car doors as soon as she gets in her car.

Harold was too old. He was over the hill.

 +

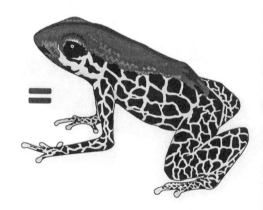 =

A distressing formula.

Practice 56 : Stress test

Directions : Underline the loudest syllable.

1. mythical 2. Goddess 3. massage 4. vigorous
5. similarity 6. fictitious 7. reinforce 8. hardship 9. dignity
10. rejection 11. accounts for 12. impress 13. oppressive
14. vitality 15. judgement 16. primary 17. threaten

Practice 57 : Stickers

Directions : Write a sticker from a story or example in the book that will help you remember what each word means. Cross out the words you already know and concentrate on those you don't.

Example: myth : Cyclops

1. mythical : _____
2. Goddess : _____
3. massage : _____
4. vigorous : _____
5. similarity : _____
6. fictitious : _____
7. reinforce : _____
8. hardship : _____
9. dignity : _____
10. rejection : _____
11. X accounts for Y : _____
12. impress upon : _____
13. harsh : _____
14. oppressive : _____
15. vitality : _____
16. judgement : _____
17. primary : _____
18. threaten : _____

Practice 58 : Using Your Own Experience

Directions : Write your own "story" and sticker to help you remember these words. If you already know a word, you don't need a sticker, of course, so write stories or examples only for those words you have trouble with.

1. mythical :
---

2. corn husk :
---

3. Goddess :
---

4. massage :
---

5. vigorous :
---

6. similarity :
---

7. fictitious :
---

8. reinforce :
---

9. hardship :
---

10. dignity :
---

11. rejection :
---

12. X accounts for Y :
---

13. impress upon :
---

14. harsh :
---

15. oppressive :
_____

16. vitality :
_____

17. judgement :
_____

18. primary :
_____

19. threaten :
_____

Practice 59 : Simple Connections

Directions : Choose a word that <u>suggests</u> the meaning of the boldfaced word. Put the appropriate letter in the blank.

a. protection **b.** fictional **c.** female **d.** rub **e.** energetic **f.** likeness
g. false **h.** emphasize **i.** difficult **j.** self-respect **k.** not accepted
l. explains **m.** important **n.** severe **o.** lack freedom **p.** liveliness **q.** decision
r. first **s.** promise harm

1. Dennis used a **fictitious** name when he signed up for the conference, so he wouldn't receive ten pounds of junk mail every day. __
2. It was a **hardship** for Charley to raise three kids without a wife. __
3. Harriet was **oppressed** by her neighbors because her dog barked all night every night. They had the wrong person. They should have oppressed her dog. __
4. John **threatened** to make Sidney horizontal. __
5. Gloria was **rejected** by the group because she had brains. Obviously, they did not. __
6. After the game, the trainer gave Joe a rub down. It was free. If Joe had gone to a **massage** parlor for the same thing, it would have cost him 50 bucks. __
7. The trainer had given Joe a **vigorous** massage. When the trainer was through, Joe knew every one of his muscles by name. __
8. A lot of people I know are going to call in sick on **Judgment** Day. __
9. The **primary** reason Mark was late for work was that his wife yanked him back into bed this morning before he could get dressed. __
10. My Greek History class is taught by a **mythical** creature whose heart is in a book and whose head is in the clouds. __
11. However, there is no **similarity** between this teacher and Cyclops. During a test, my Greek History teacher has eyes in the back of his head. __
12. Stella dressed like a recycling **goddess**. __
13. Maria unwrapped the **corn husks** from the tamales and feasted. __
14. A belly dancer's navel seems to have lots of **vitality**. __
15. The Winter was **harsh**, but the bed was warm. __
16. The manager who eliminated retiree benefits may have more status, but she has less **dignity**. __
17. ---
    Sarah: I want to **impress upon** you the importance of getting this job out on time.
    Cindy: We......
    Sarah : I cannot tell you how important it is. Work evenings if you have to, hire extra help if you need to, but get it done on time. If you do, there'll be a big bonus for you.
(Cindy thought it better not to tell Sarah that the job was already done.) __

18. The teacher **reinforced** her point by pounding on the desk, which unintentionally woke up all the students in the back row. __
19. No one could **account for** the change in Ed's lifestyle until they discovered that Ed was embezzeling money from the company. __

Practice 60 : Similarities

<u>Directions</u> : Write a word in each blank which is related to this word.

1. corn : _____   _____   _____   _____

Practice 61 : Opposites

<u>Directions</u> : Choose a word that means the opposite of the boldfaced word. Put the appropriate letter in the blank.

a. real **b.** lifeless **c.** dissimiliar
d. true **e.** play down **f.** piece of cake **g.** no respect
h. acceptance **i.** gentle **j.** free **k.** lack energy **l.** last **m.** comfort

1. The Sales Manager **reinforced** his mesage with a slide show. Some people called it a sideshow. __
2. His Uncle Stanley treated Stan **harshly**, but left him lots of money, so maybe it was worth it. __
3. Have you heard the **myth** that there is a more entertaining vocabulary book than this one? __
4. There are some **similarities** between an elephant and a field mouse. They are, for example, both gray. __
5. The neighbors **threatened** Hal with a lawsuit if he didn't stop working on his car in front of his house. They said they didn't want to come home to grease every night. __
6. Ben **rejected** his wife's suggestion that her brother move in with them. __
7. The **primary** reason he quit his job was that he was sure he was going to be fired. __
8. Dave had little **vitality** left after working overtime. __
9. Cynthia has waged a **vigorous** campaign for the Senate. At the moment, she has an even chance of winning. __
10. The hotel's air conditioning went out, so Jim and Claire avoided the **oppressive** Arizona heat by spending the afternoon in the swimming pool. __

Practice 62: Do these make sense, or not?

Directions: If the information in the sentence is consistent, if everything fits OK, if there are no contradictions, nothing improbable or impossible, then write YES in the blank. However, if the parts don't fit, if it doesn't make sense, if its ridiculous or absurd, then write NO in the blank.

1. A good **massage** can calm your nerves. __
2. The value of money was **impressed upon** Tina as she watched her husband die from liver disease because they couldn't afford to buy a replacement organ for him. __
3. Harold put the **corn husks** in the compost pile in the garden. They'll make the ground better for growing vegetables next year. __
4. Sally **reinforced** her point with a gentle suggestion. __
5. The second mortgage was the **primary** loan on their house. __
6. Larry exercised **vigorously** for an hour without sweating. __
7. **Goddesses** are not ugly. __
8. Marvin's explanation **accounted for** Freddie's absence from work yesterday. Marvin said that aliens probably came down and took Freddie to their planet for an alienburger. __
9. For no reason, George **threatened** to give me $20,000. __
10. There are a lot of **fictitious** characters in fiction. __
11. A flag pole is **diagonal**. __
12. The mother's **harsh** words made her daughter feel better. __
13. Blue eyes and brown eyes have no **similarities**. __
14. The old man had a lot of **vitality**. Every day, he walked twenty miles to the store. __
15. **Judge** others only if you have enough weapons to prevent others from judging you. __
16. The alcoholic was able to maintain his **dignity** as he lay in the pile of cow dung in the field near the road. __
17. Superman is a **mythical** character. __
18. The Princess leads a life of **hardship** in the palace - too much rich food, too many heavy jewels. __
19. Will was doubly sad. He had just been **rejected** by Stephanie and Stephanie's parrot. __
20. Paying people wages that will not allow them to support themselves is **oppression**. __

Really?
Directions: Explain your answers to these items:

4. _____
8. _____
13. _____
15. _____
16. _____
20. _____

Write

Directions: Write a sentence of your own for each of the words you are learning. Do not write sentences for words you already know. Instead, write a sentence for any substitute words you have chosen to learn.

Lesson 9 Study Guide

Word	Substitute	Similar	Opposite	Memory	✓
corn husk					
mythical					
goddess					
massage					
vigorous					
similarity					
fictitious					
reinforce					
hardship					
dignity					
rejection					
X accounts for Y					
impress upon					
harsh					
oppressive					
vitality					
judgment					
primary					
threaten					

Fairy godmothers are definitely fictitious characters.

Chapter 4

Bear this in mind. All dogs are not friendly.

Lesson 10 Focus Sheet

Word	✓	Subst Word	Listen	Speak	Read	Write
ancient						
confusion						
chaos						
Eros						
elder						
creation						
telescope						
X could be described as Y						
bear something in mind						
ignorance						
dust						
current						
vortex						
heavenly body						
all of a sudden						
century						
duplicate						
equivalent						
gravitational						
nebulous						

Lesson 10

170. ancient /en.chənt/ adj.

Opposite: modern
Meaning: If something is ancient, it is very, very old.

Example:
His dignity fell apart like ancient ruins as he became, more and more, a yes man for the boss.

Example:
The old Indian sitting in the brand new Mercedes convertible provided a wonderful contrast of the ancient and the modern.

Tip 102: **ruins** = what is left of old buildings that have fallen apart as time has passed
Tip 103: **brand new** = very new
Tip 104: **convertible** = a car with a top that can be taken down

171. confusion /kən.fyu.ʒən/ n.

Other forms: **confusing** /kən.fyu.zɪŋ/ adj. **confused** /kən.fyuzd/ adj. **confuse** /kən.fyuz/ v.
Opposite: clarity
Meaning: When people are confused, they don't know what to do. When something is confusing it is hard to understand. A state of confusion refers to a condition involving a number of people.

Example:
There was a lot of confusion immediately after the earthquake.

Example:
I'm confused. They told me to go down Main Street for four blocks, turn right, go three blocks on North Santa Cruz, and I would find the Good Earth restaurant. I've done that and there's no restaurant here.

Example:
Trying to program an old VCR is very confusing.

Tip 105: **VCR** = video cassette recorder (for recording and playing movies, etc.

172. chaos /ke.as/ n.

Other forms: **chaotic** /ke.**a**.dɪk/ adj.
Opposite: order
Meaning: There is no order when there is chaos. No order, no rules, no one in charge. There is disorder and confusion until order is restored.

Example:
There was complete chaos on the field after Brazil won the World Cup.

Example:
Things were pretty chaotic in the office after the company announced there would be layoffs of 40% of the work force.

173. Eros /ɛr.os/ n

Other forms: **erotic** /ə.**ra**.dɪk/ adj. **eroticism** /ə.**ra**.də.sɪ.zəm/ n.
Opposite (of erotic): frigid, passionless
Meaning: Eros means strong passion and desire, especially sexual desire. Erotic art is designed to heighten passion. Those who sell XXX movies sell eroticism.

Example:
Everyone in the theater was breathing heavily. The movie was very erotic.

Example:
Eros is often stronger than reason.

Tip 106: **heighten** = make it stronger
Tip 107: **reason** = the ability to think

174. elder /ɛl.dər/ adj

Other forms: **older** /ol.dər/ adj
Opposite: younger
Meaning: Elder means older, but it's a formal and old fashioned way of saying it.

Example:
His elder brother got the farm; he got nothing.

Example:
The elder women in the tribe prepared the bed for the chief's new wife, his seventeenth.

175. creation /kri.e.shən/ n.

Other forms: **create** /kri.et/ v. **creative** /kri.e.dɪv/ n.
Opposite: destruction
Meaning: *The creation* refers to the creation of the world by God. We create things when we make something new. We are creative when we do things in new ways.

Example:
The identical twins created a lot of confusion when Joan would tell everyone she was June and June would say she was Joan.

Example:
Little Lenny, who was three years old, was a very creative thinker. One day, his mother told him she had to go next door for a minute to talk to Mrs. Jones, a neighbor. Before she left, she told Lenny not to touch any of the cookies on the table because they were going to eat dinner soon. Little Lenny was very hungry and the cookies were irresistible, so he grabbed a handful of them and stuffed them into his mouth. He had just finished chewing them and swallowing them when his mom returned from Mrs. Jones's. She saw cookie crumbs on the table. She saw cookie crumbs on Little Lenny's sweatshirt. She saw cookie crumbs on Little Lenny's chin, and said, "Lenny, why did you eat those cookies when I told you not to touch them?" Little Lenny thought quickly and answered, "I didn't eat the cookies, mom. A big green monster came in through the window while you were gone and he ate 'em all up before I could stop him. Then he jumped out the window and ran away."

Tip 108: **identical** = the same; **identical twins** = two brothers or sisters born at the same time who look the same

176. telescope /tɛl.ə.skop/ n.

Other forms: **telescopic** /tɛl.ə.ska.pɪk/ adj.
Meaning: A telescope is a device for viewing (looking at) the stars, and so on. A telescopic device, however, is any instrument that can be expanded in length (made longer).

Example:
At first, Jim used the telescope to watch the stars. Later, he used it to watch Alice Jean who lived in the big white house across the street.

Example:
Abdul Rahim's body seemed telescopic as he rose above the rim to stuff the ball into the basket. Cal 91 UCLA 89. End of game.

Tip 109: **rise, rose, risen** = go up
Tip 110: **rim** = top edge of the basket ; **basket** = the goal where points are scored in basketball

177. X could be described as Y

<u>Other forms</u>: **describe** /də.skraib/ v. **description** /də.skrɪp.shən/ n.
<u>Opposite</u>: make
<u>Meaning</u>: When we tell people what something looks like or give them an idea of what it's like, we are describing it to them. Describe and *give a description of* mean the same thing. When we say that something could be described as this or that, we mean it's possible to describe it in this way.

<u>Example</u>:
Our nephew Alvin could be described as a "gentle monster". He's very thoughtful and considerate, but he told me the other day that he would be happy to go over to Nancy's boyfriend's house and beat him up if he didn't stop bugging her.

<u>Example</u>:
California Governor Pete Wilson's aborted campaign for the Presidency could be described as a wonderful catastrophe. He quit because he couldn't win, so his policies which would oppress immigrants and the poor won't be implemented, at least by him.

<u>Tip 111</u>: **bug** = bother
<u>Tip 112</u>: **aborted** = stopped, ended
<u>Tip 113</u>: **catastrophe** = disaster
<u>Tip 114</u>: **to implement** = to put into action = to put in force = to begin using

178. bear something in mind /bɛr/ Idiom

<u>Opposite</u>: forget it
<u>Meaning</u>: If you bear something in mind, you keep it in mind, you remember it, you don't forget it.

<u>Example</u>:
Bear this in mind: Your father isn't going to change, so you'll have to learn to accept him the way he is.

<u>Example</u>:
The project leader told the team, "Bear in mind that the deadline for this project is only a week away, so we'll have to put in long hours to finish it on time.

<u>Tip 115</u>: **deadline** = the time when something has to be finished
<u>Tip 116</u>: **to put long hours** = to work long hours
<u>Tip 117</u>: **on time** = when it is supposed to be finished = in time to meet the deadline. **a week away** = a week from now (a week from some date)

179. ignorance /ɪg.nor.əns/ n.

Other forms: **ignorant** /ɪg.nor.ənt/ adj.
Opposite: knowledgeable
Meaning: We are ignorant of something when we don't know about it, when we are unaware of it. That doesn't mean we are stupid. When we learn about it, we are no longer ignorant of it. Ignorance is a temporary state; stupidity is a permanent condition.

Example:
Ignorance of the law is no excuse. If you commit a crime, and you tell the judge you didn't know it was a crime, you still go to jail.

Example:
Charles was totally ignorant of her plans to divorce him.

Tip 118: We are no longer ignorant. = We are not ignorant any more. = We are not ignorant any longer.

180. dust /klaud əv dəst/ noun phrase

Other forms: **dust** /dəst/ v. **dirt** /dərt/ n. **mud** /məd/ n.
Meaning: If you are outside, and you reach down and pick up a handful of dirt from the ground, your hands will get a little dirty. If the dirt is very fine, a strong wind may produce a cloud of dust and some of the dust may blow into your eyes. If it rains, the dirt will get wet, and you'll get mud all over your shoes.

Example:
I could see that she wasn't able to take care of her house; there was dust on every piece of furniture and there were cobwebs on the ceiling.

Example:
"Dust off your old basketball uniform, John. The parents are playing the freshman next Friday night."

Tip 119: **cobweb** = spider webs filled with dust or patterns of dust formed by moisture or oil vapors which look like spider webs

181. current /kər.ənt/ adj.

Other forms: **currently** /kər.ənt.li/ adv.
Meaning: If something is current, it is happening during the present period of time, not in the past and not in the distant future. How long the present period of time is depends on the circumstances.

Example:
Company newsletters often contain a column called *Current Events*. This column in a weekly newsletter tells employees which activities are scheduled during the current week.

Example:
"The doctor is currently out of town, but he'll be back on Thursday. Would you like to make an appointment for Thursday for you broken neck?"

Tip 120: **be back** = return

182. vortex /vor.tɛks/ n.

Other forms: **vortices** /vor.tə.siz/ n. (plural)
Meaning: A whirlpool is an example of a vortex. What's a whirlpool? It's water spinning around in the middle of the river which carries things that come into it down to the bottom of the river. A vortex in space refers to clouds of dust particles, or other forms of matter, spinning around in the sky.

Example:
The outdoor sculpture consisted of a woman sitting innocently at the top of a thick wire vortex, her legs dangling down inside the rim. On the ground in the middle of the vortex was a wolf, looking up, drooling.

Tip 121: **drooling** = saliva (mouth water) was coming out of his mouth

183. heavenly body /hɛv.ən.li ba.di/ noun phrase

Other forms: **heaven** /hɛv.ən/ **the heavens** /hɛv.ənz/
Opposite (of heaven): hell
Meaning: For Christians, heaven is the place that good people go when they die. Hell is the place bad people go when they kick off. People think of heaven as being up in the sky, so heavenly bodies are planets, stars, meteors, etc. in the sky, in space, in the heavens.

Example:
The space craft moved past unnamed heavenly bodies on its way to the center of the galaxy.

Example:
Eilis looked at Brad Pitt and sighed, "He has a heavenly body."

Tip 122: **kick off** = die (very informal)
Tip 123: **galaxy** = a large group of stars

184. all of a sudden /ɔl əv ə sə.dən/ Idiom

Other forms: **suddenly** /sə.dən.li/ adv.
Opposite: slowly
Meaning: When something happens all of a sudden, it happens quickly, without warning. In other words, all of a sudden = suddenly.

Example:
The professor had been lecturing for about thirty minutes when, all of a sudden, Jane jumped up from her seat and ran out of the classroom. I saw her later that afternoon and asked her why she had left so suddenly. She told me she remembered that she had left the stove on and that she had run all the way home to turn it off.

Example:
I heard the strange noise behind me and, all of a sudden, the street went dark as the clouds passed over the moon just as the street lights went out from the power failure. I was never seen again.

Tip 124: without warning = You didn't know it was going to happen. Nobody told you. There was no sign that it was going to happen.

185. century /sɛn.chʊr.i/ n.

Meaning: The 18th Century lasted from 1700 until 1799. The "hundreds number" is always one number lower than the century.

Example:
In the 18th Century, people didn't sit watching TV all night after dinner, not because they weren't lazy, but because there were no TV's in the 18th century. If there had been, they would have been sitting and watching General Hospital.

Example:
20th Century Fox is the name of a movie studio. I wonder whether they will change their name when we enter the 21st Century.

186. duplicate /du.plə.ket/ v.

Other forms: **duplication** /du.plə.ke.shən/ n.
Meaning: To duplicate means to copy, to make another one exactly like the first one.

Example:
Grandma's recipe for split pea soup was hard to duplicate. If you made one little mistake, it would turn out lousy.

163

Example:
Despite Biotechnology and movies showing clones taking over the world, none of us can really be duplicated. We are all unique, one of a kind.

Tip 125: **turn out lousy** = **end up lousy** = be terrible when it is done
clones = copies of human beings

187. equivalent /ə.kwɪv.ə.lənt/ adj.

Other forms: **equal** /i.kwəl/ adj. (-ly adv) **equality** /i.kwal.ə.ti/ n.
Opposite (of equality): inequality
Meaning: If two things are equivalent, they are approximately the same, they are similar enough that any small differences between them are not important.

Example:
A dollar bill and 100 pennies are of equal value; they are worth the same amount; they are equivalent in value.

Example:
End up lousy and *turn out lousy* are equivalent expressions; they mean about the same thing.

Tip 126: **approximately** = about

188. gravitational /græv.ə.te.shən.əl/ adj.

Other forms: **gravity** /græv.ə.ti/ n. **gravitate** /græv.ə.tet/ v.
Meaning: Gravity refers to the magnetic pull of the earth.

Example:
The only law that crook obeyed was the law of gravity.

Example:
The professor was saying, "We walk on the ground because of the gravitational pull of the earth. Otherwise, we would float in the air." Tom was thinking, "I walk on the ground because I can't afford to buy a car."

Tip 127: **crook** = criminal

Vortex

189. nebulous /nɛ.byu.ləs/ adj.

Other forms: **nebular** /nɛ.byu.lər/ adj. **nebula** /nɛ.byu.lə/ n. (plural: nebulae)
Opposite (of nebulous): clear
Meaning: A nebula is a mass of stars and gases that are millions of miles away. One can see the light shining from it, but it is difficult to see the different forms which make up the nebula. Anything that is nebulous is *vague* and *ambiguous*; it's hard to understand or hard to see because it is unclear.

Example:
Adam's memories of his father are quite nebulous. His father left when he was two years old. He has not seen him since.

Example:
The Nebular Hypothesis was just one of the many theories attempting to explain the origin of the universe.

Tip 128: **hypothesis** = assumption based on some evidence or experience

Certainly, the monster got the cookies.

Scotty Pippen grabbed the rim.

Practice 63 : Stress test

Directions : Underline the loudest syllable.

1. ancient 2. confusion 3. chaos 4. Eros
5. elder 6. creation 7. telescope 8. describe 9. ignorant
10. current 11. vortex 12. heavenly 13. century
14. duplicate 15. equivalent 16. gravitational 17. nebulous

Practice 64 : Stickers

Directions : Write a memory sticker from a story or example in the book that will help you remember what each word means. Cross out the words you already know and concentrate on those you don't.

Example: Eros: XXX

1. ancient: _____
2. confusion: _____
3. chaos: _____
4. Eros: _____
5. elder: _____
6. creation: _____
7. telescope: _____
8. X could be described as: _____
9. bear it in mind: _____
10. ignorant: _____
11. cloud of dust: _____
12. current: _____
13. vortex: _____
14. heavenly body: _____
15. all of a sudden: _____
16. century: _____
17. duplicate: _____
18. equivalent: _____
19. gravitational: _____
20. nebulous: _____

Practice 65 : Using Your Own Experience

Directions : Write your own "story" and memory label to help you remember these words. If you already know a word, you don't need a sticker of course, so write stories or examples only for those words you have trouble with.

1. ancient :
___

2. confusion :
___

3. chaos :
___

4. Eros :
___

5. elder :
___

6. creation :
___

7. telescope :
___

8. X could be described as :
___

9. bear something in mind :
___

10. ignorant :
___

11. dust :
___

12. current :
___

13. vortex :
___

14. heavenly body :
___

15. all of a sudden :
_____

16. century :
_____

17. duplicate :
_____

18. equivalent :
_____

19. gravitational :
_____

20. nebulous :
_____
_____

Shirley focused on her goal.

Practice 66 : Simple Connections

Directions : Choose a word that <u>suggests</u> the meaning of the boldfaced word. Put the appropriate letter in the blank.

a. old b. don't know what to do c. disorder d. desire e. older f. make
g. make longer h. description i. remember j. no info k. particles
l. now m. screw n. planet o. immediately p. 100 years q. copy
r. the same s. attraction t. vague

1. Bob's **elder** brother lived in Germany when beer was ten cents. __
2. **Current** law favors awarding child custody to mothers. __
3. The Earth is also a **heavenly body**. __
4. There was no **confusion** about what the teacher meant when he said, "Shut up!" __
5. Helen's van looked **ancient,** but it was only two years old. Five kids, the kid's friends, and their huge dog all contributed. __
6. The trainer gave Joe a free rubdown. It was roughly **equivalent** to the massage at the massage parlor except for the price. __
7. John had a golf ball retriever that **telescoped** so he could reach balls he had hit in the creek. It was a good investment because he got a lot of other people's golf balls too. __
8. People are soon going to be living for more than a **century**. __
9. The **primary** reason Mike was **ignorant** was that he never bothered to find out anything. He thought he could get by on personality and uninformed opinion. __
10. As a result, his ideas were pretty **nebulous**. __
11. Mr. Estebrooks was watching a baseball game on TV when **all of a sudden** a ball came flying through the window. It landed on the kitchen floor behind him just as the TV announcer yelled, "It's gone! Home run!" __
12. There was **chaos** in the funeral parlor when the coffin creaked open, the deceased sat up and began to sing "Blue Hawaii". __
13. It's odd. **Eros** controlled his whole life, but he never found love. __
14. The atmosphere at the ad agency was so oppressive that it was almost impossible to be **creative**. __
15. I don't think anyone could **duplicate** the subtle beauty of a Seurat painting. __
16. The **gravitational** pull of the sun lured the wayward satellite closer and closer to oblivion. __
17. ---
    <u>Sarah</u>: What does June's new boyfriend look like?
    <u>Cindy</u>: Well, he **could be described as** a gorilla with a tie.
    <u>Sarah </u>: Yikes! __
18. **Vortices** are screwy. __
19. First, it was mud. The wind blew and the temperatures rose. Then it was dirt. The temperatures continued to rise and the wind blew hotter. Finally, it was **dust**. And it blew away. Like the days of youth. __
20. **Bear in mind**, though, that the end of youth is the beginning of wisdom. __

Practice 67 : Similarities

Directions: Write a word in each blank which has a meaning similar to the words given.

1. all of a sudden : _____ _____ _____
2. aborted : _____ _____
3. implement : _____ _____ _____
4. rise : _____ _____

Practice 68 : Opposites

Directions: Choose a word that means the opposite of the boldfaced word. Put the appropriate letter in the blank.

a. modern **b.** clarity **c.** order **d.** frigid **e.** destruction **f.** become shorter
g. forget **h.** knowledgeable **i.** different **j.** repulsion **k.** clear

1. I looked down at the **ancient** street in Pompeii and saw the ancient symbol, carved in the large block of paving stone, which pointed to the ancient whore houses . __
2. Uncle Stanley's opinions were consciously **nebulous**. He thought it was risky to let anyone know what he really believed. __
3. The giraffe **telescoped** its neck into the tree and yanked off a leaf with its teeth. __
4. There was **chaos** among the animals trying to escape the forest fire. __
5. **Bear this in mind** : If you don't get your degree, someone else will, and they will also get your job. __
6. Anyone who climbs mountains is testing the law of **gravity**. __
7. Paul had been offered two jobs which were essentially **equivalent**, except for the fact that one was in Cleveland and one was in Paris. Which one do you think he took? __
8. **Erotic** movies are X-rated movies, although many R-rated movies are also erotic. __
9. When it came to 3D computer graphics, Cynthia was downright **ignorant**. But she knew marketing like the back of her hand. __
10. There was some **confusion** about what the monkey wanted until he spit in George's face. __

Practice 69: Do these make sense, or not?

Directions : If the information in the sentence is consistent, if everything fits OK, if there are no contradictions, nothing improbable or impossible, then write YES in the blank. However, if the parts don't fit, if it doesn't make sense, if its ridiculous or absurd, then write NO in the blank.

1. **Chaos** can calm your nerves. __
2. Frank impressed upon his **elder** brother the necessity of visiting their rich uncle in the hospital. __
3. Jerry, an LA native, prefers to remain **ignorant** about ice hockey. __
4. **Eros** will calm your nerves. __
5. The primary pattern in her design was a square object that looked like a **vortex**. __
6. Larry pulled vigorously on the **telescope**, so it wouldn't open. __
7. Goddesses have **heavenly bodies**. __
8. Marvin's announcement of layoffs accounted for the **confusion**. __
9. At the end of the 13th **century**, in 1399, many ancient books were destroyed. __
10. **Bear in mind** that fictitious characters are not real. So put away your cape, Batman. __
11. If you drop the ball, **gravity** will pull you out of contention for the promotion. __
12. The supervisor's **nebulous** message clarified what Jon had to do. __
13. **Dust** and smoke have no **similarities**. __
14. The office workers seemed to have a lot of vitality, but **all of a sudden**, they stopped working, pulled out their make up, and started to chat about what happened on General Hospital yesterday. The boss, who had just walked through the office, had left for the day. __
15. The ancient medicine man is **currently** employed at Apple Computer. __
16. Here is Benjamin Franklin's formula for inventing clever phrases : First, steal them. Then **create** them. __
17. Myth is most often a product of **ancient** times. __
18. The Biotech scientist didn't like his wife, so he **duplicated** her. __
19. Will **could be described as** a parrotless man. __
20. Fifty bucks and 500 bucks are **equivalent**. After all, they are both money. __

Really?

Directions: Explain your answers to these items :

2. _____
4. _____
11. _____
17. _____
18. _____

Write

<u>Directions</u>: On a separate sheet, write a sentence of your own for each of the words you are learning. Do not write sentences for words you already know. Instead, write a sentence for any substitute words you have chosen to learn.

Lesson 10 Study Guide

Word	Substitute	Similar	Opposite	Memory	✓
ancient					
confusion					
chaos					
Eros					
elder					
creation					
telescope					
X could be described as Y					
bear something in mind					
ignorance					
dust					
current					
vortex					
heavenly body					
all of a sudden					
century					
duplicate					
equivalent					
gravitational					
nebulous					

Lesson 11 Focus Sheet

Word ✓	Subst Word	Listen	Speak	Read	Write
disk-shaped					
to have a lump in your throat					
a series of					
concentric					
dense					
solar					
at the turn of the century					
alternative					
unique					
probable					
trapped					
shrink					
inward					
conserve					
angular					
momentum					
circular					
whirling & twirling					
skater					
spin					

Lesson 11

190. disk-shaped /dɪsk shəpt/ adj.

Other forms: disk /dɪsk/ n.
Meaning: A disk is a flat, circular object. However, disk is also used for the rectangular floppy disks used in computer disk drives. If something is disk-shaped, it looks like a round disk, not like a 1.4 MB floppy disk, for example.

Example:
Sam put the CD-ROM disk into his compact disk drive, double-clicked on the application icon and the application started up immediately. Obviously, he was using a Macintosh.

Example:
The disk-shaped space craft had to be carrying visitors from another planet. We don't have any disk-shaped space vehicles.

Tip 129: obviously = of course

191. .i.to have a lump in your throat
/ləmp ɪn yor θrot/ Idiom

Opposite: to be confident
Meaning: When someone is very nervous, sometimes we say he has a lump in his throat.

Example:
She had a lump in her throat as she walked toward the stage to sing for the very first time in front of the large audience.

Example:
My daughter Heather almost never has a lump in her throat when she auditions for a part. Her attitude is "I'm going to go up there and make them want me."

Tip 130: audition = try out

192. a series of /ə sir.iz əv/ Measure Term

Meaning: A series of refers to a number of events performed in a sequence. If you make a series of mistakes, for example, you make a number of mistakes, one after the other. You make several mistakes in a row. You make many errors in a row.

Example:
They made a series of assumptions that were all founded on inaccurate data.

Example:
A series of errors were made in the calculations.

Tip 131: **in a row** = in a sequence, one after the other
Tip 132: **founded on** = based on

193. concentric /kən.sɛn.trɪk/ adj.

Other forms: **center** /sɛn.tər/ n.
Meaning: *Concentric* means *around the center*.

Example:
There are concentric rings around Saturn.

Example:
The brim of her hat consisted of concentric rings of color, which made her look like she had a halo. She is the last person on earth who should have a halo.

Tip 133: **ring** = Rings are circular bands.
Tip 134: **brim** = the outer band on a hat
Tip 135: **halo** = a wide band of light around someone's head; halos usually denote a holy person
Tip 136: **denote** = point to, identify

194. dense /dɛns/ adj.

Other forms: **density** /dɛns.ə.ti/ n. **denseness** /dɛns.nəs/ n.
Opposite: sparse
Meaning: Dense means packed together. Molecules are packed together tightly in an object that is very dense. In other words, the molecules in a dense object are compact; they are close to each other. The degree of compactness = its density. If we say a person is dense, we mean that person is not very intelligent.

Example:
Steve had a difficult time getting through the dense crowd.

Example:
The dense clouds hid the sun and the warmth it would have brought her during this difficult moment. He had given her a rather obvious sign that he was not interested in marriage after all.

195. solar /so.lər/ adj.

Meaning: The Spanish word for sun is *el Sol*. So now you know what solar refers to.

Example:
I put solar panels on my roof in 1978 to collect energy from the sun which now heats the water in my house. The best thing about doing that is I have never received a utility bill from the sun.

Example:
Solar energy is often used to heat swimming pools.

Tip 137: **utilities** = electricity, gas, water

196. at the turn of the century /tərn/ Idiom

Meaning: At the turn of the century refers to a period of time just before and just after one century becomes the next.

Example:
Do you realize that at the turn of the 20th century women could not vote in this country? Is that appalling or what?

Example:
Generally, people have high expectations at the turn of the century.

Tip 138: **high expectations** = We expect something to be very good.

197. alternative /al.tər.nə.tɪv/ n.

Opposite: no other choices
Meaning: *Alternative* means *choice*.

Example:
Mary said to her husband, "You have two alternatives: stop drinking or leave."

Example:
Try to make the best of the alternatives that life gives you.

198. unique /yu.nik/ adj.

Other forms: **uniqueness** /yu.**nik**.nəs/ n.
Opposite: commonplace, ordinary
Meaning: *Unique* means *one of a kind*. It may also refer to something that cannot be matched, cannot be surpassed, i.e. something that is so good it has no competition.

Example:
That diamond is unique. There is no other diamond like it.

Example:
Each of us is valuable if for no other reason than we are unique. You are the only you in the universe.

Tip 139: **if for no other reason than** = if only because

199. probable /pra.bə.bəl/ adj.

Other forms: **probability** /pra.bə.**bɪl**.ə.ti/ n.
Opposite: improbable, having a low probability
Meaning: If something is probable, there is a good likelihood that it will happen, there is a good chance that it will happen, there is a high probability that it will happen.

Example:
The average life expectancy for males in this country is 74 years. However, a fortune teller told me, among other things, that I would live to be 90. It was worth the ten bucks I gave her.

Example:
There is a low probability that I will win the California lottery, since one's chances of winning are one in fourteen million. However, there is a high probability that the sun will rise tomorrow morning, so I'm happy.

Tip 140: **among other things** = including other things = in addition to other things
Tip 141: **ten bucks** = $10.

200. trapped /træpt/ adj.

Other forms: **trap** /træp/ v. **trap** /træp/ n.
Opposite: free
Meaning: If something is trapped, it is caught; it cannot get away. A trap is a device for catching something or someone. One can *be* trapped or *feel* trapped.

Example:
We call it a mouse trap, but it isn't really a trap. It's a mouse murderer. The mouse goes for the cheese or the piece of meat and *WHAM!* the mouse is killed. But what sweet young housewife would buy one if it were called a mouse murderer.

Example:
The miners were trapped in the coal mine for two days. They just got them out a few hours ago.

Example:
Martha felt trapped. She was very unhappy in her job, but there were no other jobs available.

201. shrink, shrank, shrunk
/shrɪŋk shræŋk shrəŋk/ v.

Other forms: **shrinking** /shrɪŋk.ɪŋ/ adj.
Opposite: expand
Meaning: Something gets smaller gradually when it shrinks. It gets smaller little by little when it shrinks.

Example:
My little wife put my new sweatshirt in the wash the other day. She put the water temperature for both the wash and the rinse on hot. She put the dryer on hot. When the sweatshirt was done, it fit my cat. I now do the laundry, for fear that she would shrink my entire wardrobe if she got her hands on it.

Example:
The following week, all my wife's girlfriends shrunk their husbands' clothes.

Tip 142: **for fear that** = because I was afraid that
Tip 143: entire **wardrobe** = all my clothes

202. inward /ɪn.wərd/ adj./adv.

Opposite: outward
Meaning: Inward refers to something that is inside, internal, interior.

Example:
When times got rough, he looked inward for strength. (He looked inside himself.)

Example:
Eben derived inner peace from sitting by the river, alone with the redwood trees and the birds and butterflies.

Tip 144: **rough** = tough = difficult = hard

203. conserve /kən.sərv/ v.

Other forms: **conservation** /kan.sər.ve.shən/ n.
Opposite: destroy
Meaning: *Conserve* and *preserve* have similar meanings. They both mean to protect, or safeguard something. *To conserve* also means *to save*.

Example:
We need to conserve natural resources such as the rain forests of Central and South America.

Example:
Our family conserves energy by doing some rather simple things, such as turning off lights when we leave a room.

204. angular /æŋ.gyu.lər/ adj.

Other forms: **angle** /æŋ.gəl/ n.
Meaning: If something is angular, it contains an angle. Angles are formed from lines that converge at any point between 0 to 360 degrees.

Example:
The two rivers converged at a 45 degree angle.

Example:
Joan had a rather large, angular nose. It pointed away from her face at a surprising angle for an alarming distance.

Tip 145: **converge** = join, come together. **alarming** = very surprising

205. momentum /mo.mɛn.təm/ n.

Meaning: Momentum refers to pace, speed, velocity, tempo, to how fast something is moving. In addition to increasing speed, momentum also refers to rising encouragement.

Example:
Their business had reached the momentum stage: sales were increasing very rapidly and profits were rising.

Example:
The teacher's praise gave Tim the momentum to continue in college while he worked at a full time job.

Tip 146: **praise** = approval.

206. circular /sər.kyu.lər/ adj.

Other forms: **circle** /sər.kəl/ n.
Meaning: *Circular* means *like a circle.*

Example:
Kelly is not a terrible driver, but she has had a hard time backing out of the driveway, but she doesn't have to worry about that anymore. Her new house has a circular driveway. A rather expensive solution to her driving problem, however.

Example:
One of life's great truths: Lifesavers are circular.

207. whirling and twirling
/wɜrl.lɪŋ ən twɜrl.lɪŋ/ adj.

Other forms: whirl /wɜrl/ v. twirl /twɜrl/ v.
Meaning: Both whirl and twirl mean to spin around.

Example:
The $100 bill that dropped from Sharon's purse into the river went whirling and twirling around in the whirlpool until it disappeared from sight.

Tip 147: disappeared from sight = She couldn't see it anymore.

208. skater /ske.dər/ n.

Other forms: skate /sket/ v.
Meaning: This is a tough one. A skater is someone who skates. An ice skater skates on ice. A roller skater uses roller skates.

Example:
Tonya Harding was a skater whose career was ruined by her stupidity.

Example:
Albert was skating on the lake when, all of a sudden, the ice broke and he fell into the cold water.

209. spin /spɪn/ (past: spun) v.

Other forms: spinning /spɪn.ɪŋ/ adj.
Meaning: When you spin around, you go around in circles. When I do that, I get dizzy.

Example:
Henry got dizzy spinning around on the dance floor.

Example:
When the truck hit the van, it spun around and crashed into the brand new Mercedes that was parked in front of Macy's.

Tip 148 dizzy = light headed. I feel like I'm going to faint, to pass out, to become unconscious.

Practice 70 : Stress test

Directions : Underline the loudest syllable.

1. series 2. concentric 3. solar 4. alternative
5. unique 6. probable 7. inward 8. conserve 9. angular
10. momentum 11. circular 12. whirling 13. twirling
14. skater

Practice 71 : Stickers

Directions : Write a sticker from a story or example in the book that will help you remember what each word means. Cross out the words you already know and concentrate on those you don't.

Example: angular : <u>Joan's nose</u>

1. disk-shaped: _____
2. lump in one's throat: _____
3. a series of: _____
4. concentric: _____
5. dense: _____
6. solar: _____
7. at the turn of the century: _____
8. alternative: _____
9. unique: _____
10. probable: _____
11. trapped: _____
12. shrink: _____
13. inward: _____
14. conserve: _____
15. angular: _____
16. momentum: _____
17. circular: _____
18. whirling & twirling: _____
19. skater: _____
20. spin: _____

This hat has a wide brim.

Practice 72 : Using Your Own Experience

Directions : Write your own "story" and sticker to help you remember these words. If you already know a word, you don't need a sticker, of course, so write stories or examples only for those words you have trouble with.

1. disk-shaped :
_____
_____

2. a lump in your throat :
_____
_____

3. a series of :
_____
_____

4. concentric :
_____
_____

5. dense :
_____
_____

6. solar :
_____
_____

7. at the turn of the century :
_____
_____

8. alternative :
_____
_____

9. unique :
_____
_____

10. probable :
_____
_____

11. trapped :
_____
_____

12. shrink :
_____
_____

13. inward :
_____
_____

14. conserve :
_____
_____

15. angular :
_____
16. momentum :
_____
17. circular :
_____
18. whirling and twirling :
_____
19. skater :
_____
20. spin :
_____
_____

Stella is the last person on earth you would expect to have a halo.

185

Practice 73 : Simple Connections

Directions : Choose a word that <u>suggests</u> the meaning of the boldfaced word. Put the appropriate letter in the blank.

a. CD b. nervous c. a number of d. center e. compact f. sun
g. change h. choice i. one j. likely k. caught l. get smaller m. internal
n. save o. angle p. speed q. circle r. spin s. person t. around and around

1. Bob had **a lump in his throat** as he picked up the phone to ask the boss for a raise. __
2. The **momentum** of the harsh storm was building as it ripped across the state. __
3. The ancient-looking Indian had an **angular**, leathery face. He was beautiful. __
4. Art said, "Finder's keepers, loser's weepers." So Dick threatened to inflict **a series of** punches on Art's nose if Art did not return the ring John had lost. __
5. Melody was rejected by the group just because she had a **disk-shaped** head. Sometimes, life is cruel. __
6. The skater was **whirling and twirling** on the ice when they announced free popcorn in the lobby. A few seconds later the whirling and twirling skater was the only person left in the rink. __
7. The skater **spun** around one more time and went to the lobby for some popcorn, too. __
8. A lot of people I know are going to call in sick on the day they are supposed to die. The others are **probably** going to be on vacation. __
9. The primary reason for **conserving** energy now is that our grandchildren will freeze to death in the winter if we don't. __
10. Aunt Agatha lost some of her dignity when she got **trapped** in the bathroom when the door stuck. __
11. There is no similarity between a **circular** shape and a pyramidal shape. __
12. Stella's clothing is always **dense**. She's wearing six layers today. __
13. A series of **concentric** rings surround Saturn. __
14. Originally, the baby's navel was an *outie*, but eventually, it shrunk into an *innie*. __
15. Kicking his son out of the house was harsh, but his son's behavior left him with no other **alternative**. __
16. Phil loved the **uniqueness** of each of his children. __
17. **At the turn of the century**, there were no mini vans, no campers, no pick-up trucks, no convertibles, no station wagons, no sports cars, no four-door sedans, and no stretch limos, but there was a heck of a lot of horse manure. __
18. The teacher reinforced her point that, although the woman in the story was not pretty, if one looked **inward**, one could see an inner beauty that was remarkable. __
19. The lack of a powerful enough **solar** battery accounts for the absence of solar-powered cars on the freeway. __

Practice 74 : Similarities

<u>Directions</u> : Write a word in each blank which has a meaning similar to the words given.

1. shrink : _____ _____
2. rough : _____ _____ _____
3. conserve : _____ _____ _____

Practice 75 : Opposites

<u>Directions</u> : Choose a word that means the opposite of the boldfaced word. Put the appropriate letter in the blank.

a. confident **b.** sparse **c.** stuck **d.** common **e.** not likely **f.** free
g. become larger **h.** outward **i.** destroy **j.** stopped

1. The Sales Manager reinforced his warning that there would be no **alternative** to increased sales with a circular movement of his index finger. __
2. Uncle Stanley was **unique**. __
3. Harvey looked **inward** for answers. __
4. The elephant kept **shrinking** and shrinking until it became a field mouse. It was trying to get a new perspective on life. __
5. Melvin had **a lump in his throat** as he asked her for his ring back. __
6. Ben suggested that his brother-in-law could move to the **dense** jungles of the Amazon. __
7. The primary reason he didn't ask Melissa to the dance was that it was **probable** that she would laugh in his face. __
8. The sales force had little **momentum** after they lost the huge contract. __
9. A terrible thing happened to Little Lenny. He got **trapped** in the ice cream parlor when they locked the doors, not knowing that Little Lenny was in there. They found him the next morning ten pounds heavier with a big smile and 29 flavors of ice cream on his face. __
10. The hotel's power went out, so they started up the generator and sent a note to all the guests asking them to **conserve** energy until the power returned. Judging from the note, I guess the guests could use it like crazy after the power was back on. __

Practice 76: Do these make sense, or not?

Directions: If the information in the sentence is consistent, if everything fits OK, if there are no contradictions, nothing improbable or impossible, then write YES in the blank. However, if the parts don't fit, if it doesn't make sense, if its ridiculous or absurd, then write NO in the blank.

1. Planning is an **alternative** to chaos. __
2. A **circular** saw has a round blade. __
3. **Solar** winds blew across the earth that afternoon. __
4. The **skater** glided across the roller rink and crashed into the deli counter. __
5. George had **a lump in his throat** because he was so confident. __
6. Larry did **a series of** vigorous exercises and then passed out on the couch. __
7. Goddesses are not very good **skaters**. __
8. The **density** of the material accounted for its weight. __
9. Murray felt **trapped** as he looked at the huge pile of work on his desk. __
10. The sweater was too small, so she had to **shrink** it. __
11. Einstein was **probably** a scientist. __
12. The car's **momentum** increased as it stopped. __
13. You are unique most of the time. __
14. The old man stood there motionless, **whirling and twirling**. __
15. A target consists of **concentric** circles around a bullseye. __
16. A **disk-shaped** object is angular, of course. __
17. Superman is **unique**. __
18. You are **spinning** if you are whirling, but not if you are twirling. __
19. Rich people have been able to **conserve** their money. __
20. Shelly breathed **inward** when she was surprised by the cat. __

Really?
Directions: Explain your answers to these items :

7. _____
9. _____
19. _____
20. _____

Write
Directions: Write a sentence of your own for each of the words you are learning. Do not write sentences for words you already know. Instead, write a sentence for any substitute words you have chosen to learn.

Lesson 11 Study Guide

Word	Substitute	Similar	Opposite	Memory	✓
disk-shaped					
to have a lump in your throat					
a series of					
concentric					
dense					
solar					
at the turn of the century					
alternative					
unique					
probable					
trapped					
shrink					
inward					
conserve					
angular					
momentum					
circular					
whirling & twirling					
skater					
spin					

Lesson 12 Focus Sheet

Word	✓	Subst Word	Listen	Speak	Read	Write
paradox						
oxymoron						
astronomy						
prototype						
condense						
thermal						
gaseous						
radiate						
sphere						
cool						
to storm out						
grain						
to be half right						
compound						
split up						
coherent						
comprehend						

Lesson 12

210. paradox /pɛr.ə.daks/ n.

Other forms: **paradoxical** /pɛr.ə.**dak**.sə.kəl/ n.
Opposite: make
Meaning: A paradox is a contradiction, an incongruity that is difficult to understand. It refers to things that are together which cannot logically be together.

Example:
How can Luke make so much money and be so dumb? That's a real paradox.

Example:
When Sue came into the office, she saw Shirley at her desk crying, so she asked Shirley what was wrong. The conversation went like this:
Shirley: It's Paul again. I hate him!
Sue: Well, if he treats you so badly, why don't you leave him?
Shirley: I can't.
Sue: Why not?
Shirley: I love him!
Now that's a paradox.

Tip 149: **incongruity** = They don't fit.
Tip 150: **dumb** = stupid

211. .i.oxymoron /ak.si.mor.an/ n.

Meaning: Oxymoron is a term I've thrown in so you can impress your friends and enemies. They'll think your English is super. They'll also think you are more intelligent than you are. All you have to say is, "Oh, that's an oxymoron." Pretty simple, huh? Now what is an oxymoron? It's a term which refers to self-contradicting phrases with the formula X + Y cannot = X + Y.

Example:
Here is an example of an oxymoron: an **honest politician**. Honest and politician cannot, of course, be used together (the skeptic says) because politicians are not honest.

Example:
Here are a few more oxymorons: an **inexpensive attorney**, a **painless dentist, an easy statistics class.**

212. astronomy /ə.stran.ə.mi/ n.

Other forms: **astronomical** /æs.trə.nam.ə.kəl/ adj.
Opposite (of astronomical): very low
Meaning: Astronomy is the study of stars, planets, suns and moons, so it makes sense that astronomical means very, very high.

Example:
George told me the other day, "I took astronomy because the college catalog said it was the study of heavenly bodies, but all I saw was stars and planets. Boy was I disappointed."

Example:
Jackie: Did you buy that coat you were talking about?
Claire: No, the price was astronomical. Can you believe they wanted $4,000 for a rabbit coat!

213. prototype /pro.do.taip/ n.

Meaning: A prototype is an original model of something. It's the very first example of something that may be produced in quantity later.

Example:
A prototype of the Copland operating system was shown at the Mac World Convention in San Francisco.

Example:
Enemy spies stole the prototype of the secret laser weapon. They were taking it back to their country when they were caught. If they had not been caught, the enemy would have been able to produce many of these weapons.

Tip 150: **spy** = secret agents who try to obtain (get) information from the enemy or the competition
Tip 151: **enemy** = the opposite of enemy is **friend**

214. condense /kən.dɛns/ v.

Other forms: **condensation** /kan.dɛn.se.shən/ n.
Opposite: diffuse
Meaning: When something is condensed, it is concentrated, compressed, compacted. When something is condensed, it becomes smaller. It takes up less room, less area, because it's density has increased.

Example:
The teacher told Brian, "You need to condense your speech. You can't talk for three hours. The audience will fall asleep."

Example:
The fog condensed on the trees, forming silver drops of water that hung on the branches.

215. thermal /θɜr.məl/ adj.

Other forms: **therm** /θɜrm/ n.
Meaning: A therm is a unit of heat, so thermal refers to heat.

Example: The thermal tiles protected the spacecraft from the intense heat that accompanies re-entry into the earth's atmosphere.

Example:
Jake: I'm going down to the corner to pick up some bread.
Phyllis: Aren't you going to be cold? It's snowing out there.
Jake: No Honey, I'll be fine. I'm wearing my thermal underwear.

Example:
Mom got the thermal blankets out and put them on each bed for the winter.

Tip 152: **accompany** = go with, occur or happen with

216. gaseous /gæ.shəs/ adj.

Other forms: **gas** /gæs/ n.
Meaning: Gaseous = like a gas.

Example:
Scientists don't know much about the gaseous forms in that galaxy.

Example:
The gaseous fumes rose from the ink bottle which sat on the shelf near the classroom window. At first Mr. Doyle, the hated English teacher, didn't notice it, but the smell of the sulfur soon became quite obvious. After a time, the teacher discovered the source and threw the bottle out the window. It landed at the feet of the principal. We heard the principal shouting at Mr. Doyle that afternoon. Another chemistry experiment well done.

Tip 153: **fumes** = gas, vapor
Tip 154: **the hated English teacher** = the students hated him
Tip 155: **after a time** = after some time had passed = later

217. radiate /re.di.et/ v.

Other forms: **radiation** /re.di.e.shən/ n. (-ed/-ing adj)
Meaning: Radiate means to spread out from some source.

Example:
The sun radiates light and heat.

Example:
Carol radiates warmth when she enters a room. She's one of the most friendly people I know.

218. sphere /sfir/ n.

Other forms: **spherical** /sfir.ə.kəl/ adj.
Meaning: A sphere is a round 3D object like a ball.

Example:
The little boy looked up at the sphere in the night sky and turned to his grandfather, "I see the rabbit, Grampa, I see the rabbit on the moon!"

Example:
The sphere flew off his bat and sailed into the air. "Oh no," one boy groaned as they all watched the baseball crash into Mr. Estebrooks living room window.

Tip 156: **-al and -ar** are often used with adjectives of shape: **spherical, octagonal/ rectangular, triangular.**

219. cool /kʊl/ adj.

Other forms: **cold** /kold/ adj.
Opposite: warm
Meaning: The opposite of hot is cold; the opposite of cool is warm. Cool is not as cold as cold and warm is not as hot as hot.

Example:
The cool weather was refreshing after the two-week hot spell.

Example:
When he smiled, she did not smile back. She was cool toward him. They had had a fight.

Tip 157: **refreshing** = stimulating. It gave them more energy, made them feel a lot better.
Tip 158: **hot spell** = a period of time when the weather is very hot

220. storm out /storm aut/ v.

Meaning: To storm out means to leave very angrily.

Example:
She stormed out of the room after he had insulted her.

Example:
After pounding on the table to emphasize how badly the sales force had done that month, the sales manager stormed out of the meeting. He had concluded earlier that a little fear might increase the sales effort.

221. grain /gren/ n.

Other forms: **granule** /græn.yəl/ n.
Meaning: A granule is a small particle or fragment or piece of something. Grain and granule are often used to mean the same thing.

Example:
NASA found grains of gold dust on the astronaut's boots. But his wife made a greater scientific discovery. She found lipstick on his collar. Now we know there is life on other planets!

222. to be half right /hæf rait/ Idiom

Meaning: If you are half right, you are partly right and partly wrong.

Example:
Joe: You can't resist me, can you?
Shelly: Well, you're half right.
Joe: What do you mean?
Shelly: I can't resist telling you what a jerk you are.

223. compound /kam.paund/ n.

Meaning: A compound is a mixture, or blend, of two or more substances.

Example:
The chemistry teacher found a simple way to demonstrate compounds to her class when she looked down at her coffee cup. The next day she came to class with a thermos of coffee and a carton of milk. She blended the two in front of the class before she drank it.

Example:
A bloody Mary is a compound: part vodka, part tomato juice.

Tip 159: Look at this sentence. **Nor does it account for the sizes of these planets.** It means **It doesn't explain the size of the planets either.**

224. split up /splɪt əp/ v.

Opposite: combine, connect
Meaning: To split up means to separate, to divide into parts. It is also used when two lovers or a married couple separate.

Example:
The meteor split up into numerous parts, one of which is heading toward the earth right now!

Example:
Ted and Nancy split up after ten years of marriage.

Tip 160: **numerous** = many
Tip 161: **headed toward** = went in the direction of
Tip 162: **data** = information. Pieces of data = pieces of information.

225. coherent /ko.hir.ənt/ adj.

Other forms: **coherence** /ko.hir.əns/ n.
Opposite: incoherent
Meaning: If something is coherent, it is understandable because its parts, pieces, or elements are consistent.

Example:
The message was incoherent; we couldn't make sense out of it.

Example:
I would say the plan is quite coherent. Everything fits together pretty well.

Tip 163: **element** = part

226. comprehend /kam.pri.hɛnd/ v.

Other forms: **comprehensive** /kam.pri.hɛn.sɪv/ n.
Opposite: incomprehensible
Meaning: If you comprehend something, you understand it. If something is comprehensible it is understandable. However, comprehensive has a different meaning. If something is comprehensive, it is complete; it includes all necessary elements.

Example:
The letter was vague and ambiguous. Actually, it was totally incoherent, so, obviously, I couldn't comprehend it.

Example:
We are not even close to comprehending the mysteries of the universe.

Tip 164: mysteries = secrets

Practice 77 : Stress test

Directions : Underline the loudest syllable.

1. paradox 2. oxymoron 3. astronomy 4. prototype
5. condense 6. thermal 7. gaseous 8. radiate 9. compound
10. coherent 11. comprehend

Practice 78 : Stickers

Directions : Write a sticker from a story or example in the book that will help you remember what each word means. Cross out the words you already know and concentrate on those you don't.

Example: thermal : thermal underwear

1. paradox : _____
2. oxymoron : _____
3. astronomy : _____
4. prototype : _____
5. condense : _____
6. thermal : _____
7. gaseous : _____
8. radiate : _____
9. sphere : _____
10. cool : _____
11. storm out : _____
12. grain : _____
13. half-right : _____
14. compound : _____
15. split up : _____
16. coherent : _____
17. comprehend : _____

Practice 79 : Using Your Own Experience

Directions : Write your own "story" and sticker to help you remember these words. If you already know a word, you don't need a sticker of course, so write stories or examples only for those words you have trouble with.

1. paradox :
   _____
   _____

2. oxymoron :
   _____

3. astronomy :
   _____

4. prototype :
   _____

5. condense :
   _____

6. thermal :
   _____

7. gaseous :
   _____

8. radiate :
   _____

9. sphere :
   _____

10. cool :
    _____

11. storm out :
    _____

12. grain :
    _____

13. half-right :
    _____

14. compound :
    _____
    _____

15. split up :
_____
_____
16. coherent :
_____
_____
17. comprehend :
_____
_____

Practice 80 : Simple Connections

Directions : Choose a word that <u>suggests</u> the meaning of the boldfaced word. Put the appropriate letter in the blank.

a. contradiction **b.** impossible **c.** not as cold as cold **d.** ball **e.** spread out **f.** gas **g.** heat **h.** concentrated **i.** original **j.** stars **k.** leave
l. granule **m.** understand **n.** consistent **o.** separate **p.** mixture **q.** partly

1. Phil's joy was **compounded** with the birth of each child. __
2. John's father told him to major in **astronomy** because his head was always in the clouds. __
3. They had to change their plans after the company Vice President died demonstrating the **prototype** of the new lightweight bullet proof vest. __
4. Rain is an example of **condensation**. __
5. Gloria **stormed out** of the room when the other managers would not listen to her suggestions. __
6. She couldn't **comprehend** why a female manager was so threatening to them. __
7. Even one **grain** of kryptonite made Superman weak. __
8. My wife wears **thermal** underwear in the winter. __
9. The Jello **cooled** in the refrigerator as Marcie made the batter for the cookies. __
10. The **gaseous** cloud above the town was created by the chemical factory. __
11. Your head is a **sphere**. __
12. A wood burning stove **radiates** heat. __
13. ---
    <u>Gary</u>: Karen's smart, isn't she?
    <u>Nancy</u> : Well, you're **half-right**. She's a smart ass. __
14. An efficient consultant is an **oxymoron**. __
15. Susan didn't have a **coherent** idea in her head. __
16. Here's a **paradox** for you to think about :
When Paul reached the top, he hit his bottom. __
17. ---
    <u>Sarah</u>: Did you hear that Hal and Maxine **split up**?
    <u>Cindy</u>: Yeah, I was really surprised.
    <u>Sarah</u> : You're kidding! They had been having trouble for years. __

Practice 81 : Similarities

<u>Directions</u> : Write a word in each blank which has a meaning similar to the words given.

1. data : _____   _____   _____
2. condense : _____   _____   _____
3. numerous : _____
4. gas : _____   _____

Practice 82 : Opposites

<u>Directions</u> : Choose a word that means the opposite of the boldfaced word. Put the appropriate letter in the blank.

a. perfect fit **b.** diffuse **c.** cold **d.** concentrated **e.** warm **f.** come back
g. unmixed **h.** combine **i.** inconsistent **j.** incomprehensible

1. Can you think of an example of an **paradox**? __
2. The gaseous mass **split** into two bodies. __
3. Harvey's problems were **compounded** when he lost his paycheck in Las Vegas. __
4. Uncle Stanley **stormed out** of the bank when they would not take his $5,000 in pennies. __
5. Jeremiah played **cool** jazz in the basement of the old night club. __
6. The liquid **condensed** into a thick syrup after simmering on the stove for an hour. __
7. Light **radiated** from the mysterious hole in the ground. __
8. The **thermal** tiles on the space craft protected it from the blistering temperatures of re-entry. __
9. The City Council was looking for a **coherent** approach to solving the problems related to teenage gangs. __
10. "I **comprehend** everything you have said," said the professor. "Unfortunately, I disagree with every bit of it." __

"A wealthy bag lady" is an oxymoron.

Practice 83: Do these make sense, or not?

Directions: If the information in the sentence is consistent, if everything fits OK, if there are no contradictions, nothing improbable or impossible, then write YES in the blank. However, if the parts don't fit, if it doesn't make sense, if its ridiculous or absurd, then write NO in the blank.

1. An oxymoron is an inconsistent **compound**. __
2. Bill didn't understand the directions; he didn't **comprehend** them. __
3. Harold's plan was **cohesive**, except for the fact that it was disorganized. __
4. **Oxymorons** are stupid. __
5. The plan was **incoherent**. We understood almost all of it. __
6. The beauty queen from the small town was really sort of ugly. Do you think that's a **paradox**? __
7. The marketing department asked manufacturing to make another dozen **prototypes** of the underwater vehicle. __
8. It was blistering hot that day, so Marvin wore his **thermal** jacket to the beach. __
9. You can't put a **sphere** in a square hole. __
10. The room **cooled** after we turned off the heater. __
11. Gas is **gaseous**. __
12. If you want to learn about the earth's surface, study **astronomy**. __
13. There isn't a **grain** of truth to what she says. It's totally false. __
14. If you're **half-right**, then you're wrong. __
15. Shirley **stormed out** of the courtroom after the judge refused to triple the support payments she was getting from her ex-husband. __
16. When the gang member attacked Ted, Ted **split** into two and pounded the gang member from the front and the back at the same time. __
17. In the early morning, there is **condensation** on the dining room table. __
18. Pamela **radiated** wealth as she entered the ballroom, her diamond and ruby necklace against her designer gown, her diamond and ruby tiara on her head, the 5 caret diamond ring on her finger - all twinkling in the light of the chandeliers. __

Really?
Directions: Explain your answers to these items :

1. _____
3. _____
4. _____
6. _____
14. _____
16. _____

Write

<u>Directions</u>: Write a sentence of your own for each of the words you are learning. Do not write sentences for words you already know. Instead, write a sentence for any substitute words you have chosen to learn.

Lesson 12 Study Guide

Word	Substitute	Similar	Opposite	Memory	✓
paradox					
oxymoron					
astronomy					
prototype					
condense					
thermal					
gaseous					
radiate					
sphere					
cool					
to storm out					
grain					
to be half right					
compound					
split up					
coherent					
comprehend					

Chapter 5

Their divorce was inevitable.

Lesson 13 Focus Sheet

Word	✓	Subst Word	Listen	Speak	Read	Write
to put it bluntly						
dishonest						
to tell the truth						
to beat around the bush						
photographer						
beak						
monk						
obsessed						
to make a fortune						
conflicting views						
inevitable						
eventual						
infinite						
unethical						
demand						
humanity						
to perfect						
on the one hand						
on the other hand						
misanthrope						

Lesson 13

227. To put it bluntly /blənt.li/ Idiom

Other forms: **blunt** /blənt/ adj.
Opposite (of blunt): subtle, tactful, polite
Meaning: When I am blunt, I am too direct, so direct that I embarrass or anger the person I'm talking to. Being blunt often makes people uneasy, uncomfortable, so it is very often considered impolite. Beginning a statement by saying *to put it bluntly* is a way of telling someone that (1) you are going to be blunt and (2) that you want to be blunt.

Example:
Jack: So when are you going to come over to my apartment and see my new painting?
Jill: Well, to put it bluntly Jack, I'll do that when hell freezes over.

Example:
Kathy: How do you like my new dress?
Ken: God, it looks real ugly on you!
Kathy (sarcastically): Thanks for being so blunt. Don't you think you could be a little more subtle?
Ken: All right, how's this? Honey, that dress just isn't your style. You are far too beautiful to wear a dress like that.
Kathy: That's more like it!

Tip 165: Since hell is supposed to be extremely hot, there is no chance that it will freeze over (completely). Thus, there is no chance that you will find Jill at Jack's apartment.
Tip 166: We often mean the opposite of what we say when we are being sarcastic.

228. dishonest /dɪs.an.əst/ adj.

Other forms: **dishonesty** /dɪs.an.əs.ti/ n. (-ly adv)
Opposite: honest
Meaning: Dishonest people don't tell the truth; they lie. They may also cheat people and steal things.

Example:
The investigation showed that the best thing we can say about the CFO is that he is dishonest. Authorities believe that he is now somewhere in the Caribbean with the $3,000,000 he stole from the employee pension fund.

Example:
Dishonesty never pays in the long run. It may not pay even in the short term since it quietly eats away at one's character, at one's inner peace, at one's sense of freedom.

<u>Tip 168</u>: **in the long run** = over time = in the end = eventually
<u>Tip 169</u>: **in the short term** = the opposite of i*n the long run*

229. To tell the truth /truθ/ Idiom

<u>Other forms</u>: **truth** /truθ/ n. **true** /tru/ adj.
<u>Opposite</u>: to lie
<u>Meaning</u>: To tell the truth means about the same thing as *actually, honestly, really.*

<u>Example</u>:
Phil: How do you like the new paint job?
Eben: To tell the truth, I've never seen a house quite as pink as that. Are you expecting Barbie to move in?

<u>Example</u>:
Frank: Now that Marcie and I have split up, tell me what you really thought of her.
Mike: Well, to tell the truth, I thought she was pretty selfish.

<u>Tip 170</u>: *Are you expecting Barbie* (Barbie Doll) *to move in?* is sarcastic.

230. to beat around the bush /bush/ Idiom

<u>Opposite</u>: to get to the point
<u>Meaning</u>: If you beat around the bush, you don't get to the point, you don't say what you want to say, you don't say what the main message is.

<u>Example</u>:
Mayor Thomas is always beating around the bush. He never tells you what he is really going to do to solve the problems of this city.

<u>Example</u>:
Stop beating around the bush and get to the point, damn' it!

231. photographer /fə.ta.grə.fər/ n.

<u>Other forms</u>: **photography** /fə.ta.grə.fi/ n. **photograph** /fo.də.græf/ n.
<u>Meaning</u>: A photographer is a person who takes photographs, of course, and photography is his or her profession. Notice how different the pronunciation of photograph is from photographer and photography.

<u>Example</u>:
Helen is majoring in photography. She's having a lot of fun taking pictures and editing them on her computer. What a great way to get a degree!

<u>Example</u>:
A photograph of the missing woman was found in the back seat of the suspect's car.

Tip 171: **suspect** = the person the police think committed the crime

232. beak /bik/ n.

Meaning: We think of a beak as a bird's mouth, but it's something like a mouth-nose combination. When we use *beak* to refer to humans, it means their nose.

Example:
As much as the worm wiggled, it could not escape the robin's beak.

Example:
When she was in deep thought, her tiny, compact lips formed a tight triangle resembling a finch's beak.

Tip 172: **wiggle** = move back and forth quickly and irregularly
Tip 173: **escape** = get away
Tip 174: **robin** = a bird
Tip 175: **finch** = a small bird

233. monk /mənk/ n.

Other forms: **monastery** /man.ə.stɛr.i/ n.
Meaning: A monk is a person who devotes his or her life to praying and studying in order to become more spiritual. Monks live in monasteries.

Example:
During the Dark Ages of Europe, you could attend a book burning party almost every Friday night - almost any night, as a matter of fact. Most of the books which survived the book burnings were hidden away in monasteries by the monks.

Example:
The thief, thinking that the monk was easy prey, attempted to rob him. He didn't know that the monk had practiced Tai Kwan Do for many years to improve his discipline.

Tip 176: **easy prey** = an easy target

234. obsessed /əb.sɛst/ adj.

Other forms: **obsession** /əb.sɛ.shən/ n.
Opposite: disinterested
Meaning: People who are obsessed with something may not be able to think of anything else. At the very least, their obsession takes up much of their time and attention. They spend too much time thinking about it.

Example:
Dave was obsessed with passing the CPA exam. He couldn't think of anything else.

Example:
An alcoholic is obsessed with alcohol. A workaholic is obsessed with work. My sister Ellan is a chocoholic. Chocolate is her only obsession.

235. to make a fortune /for.chən/ Idiom

Other forms: **fortune** /for.chən/ n.
Opposite: go broke
Meaning: When you make a fortune, you become very rich since a fortune is a hell of a lot of money.

Example:
Joe Kennedy made his fortune selling whiskey.

Example:
If you're very lucky, you can win a fortune in the California lottery.

236. conflicting views /kən.flɪk.tɪŋ vyuz/ Noun Phrase

Other forms: **conflict** /kən.flɪkt/ v. **conflict** /kan.flɪkt/ n.
Opposite: compatible views
Meaning: When people have conflicting views, they are in disagreement with each other; they disagree about something; they have opposing views.

Example:
The high school friends just couldn't get along as adults; they had conflicting views about too many things.

Example:
Sue: I'm sorry I can't meet you in Chicago next week, Stan. I have a scheduling conflict. I'll be in New York for the next three weeks setting up our new office. Let's try to get together back in San Francisco at the end of the month.
Stan: At the end of the month in San Francisco is fine. See you then.

Tip 177: Notice the noun **conflict** and the verb **conflict**. In word pairs following this pattern, the noun is stressed on the 1st syllable and the verb is stressed on the 2nd, e.g.
protest : /pro.tɛst/ /prə.tɛst/ **combat** /kam.bæt/ /kəm.bæt/

237. inevitable /ɪn.ɛv.ɪ.də.bəl/ adj.

Opposite: It won't happen.
Meaning: If something is inevitable, it is bound to happen; it is certain to happen; it is guaranteed to happen; it is going to happen for sure. There is no way to stop it from happening.

Example:
Their divorce was inevitable. I have never seen two people fight that much.

Example:
There are two things in life that are inevitable: death and taxes.

238. eventual /i.vɛn.chu.əl/ adj.

Other forms: **eventually** /i.vɛn.chu.əl.li/ adv.
Meaning: If something will happen eventually, it will happen sooner or later. *Eventual* suggests inevitability.

Example:
The eventual fall of the Roman Empire left Europe in chaos.

Example:
Betty: I'll never understand chemistry!
Eilis: Sure you will, Betty. You'll get it eventually.

Example:
Harriet: Emma, I'm getting worried about him. He's still standing there in the rain.
Emma: Why doesn't he go home where it's dry?
Harriet: He said he's going to stand there until I agree to marry him.
Emma: Don't worry about it. He'll go home eventually.

239. infinite /ɪn.fə.nət/ adj.

Other forms: **infinitely** /ɪn.fə.nət.li/ adv.
Opposite: finite /fai.nait/
Meaning: Anything that is infinite will last forever, or seem to last forever. However, infinitely = very, very.

Example:
Maude has infinite patience with her son Bobby. If I were her, I would have spanked him a long time ago.

Example:
A Honda Accord is infinitely better than an Izuzu. Of course, it's also more expensive.

240. unethical /ən.ɛ.θɪ.kəl/ adj.

Other forms: **ethical** /ɛ.θɪ.kəl/ adj
Opposite: ethical
Meaning: An unethical person is dishonest. A very unethical person is corrupt. An ethical person tries to treat people fairly, tries to do what is right.

Example:
It was unethical for Jason to pay Sherry to write his research paper for him. It was also stupid. Sherry can't write worth a damn'.

Example:
Dennis: Guess what. I just got my bank statement and it says I have $450,067 in my account, but I know I have only $67 in there.
George: Wow! You're rich! Bank error in your favor. Collect 450,000 bucks!
Dennis: I wish I could. Damn' it, why am I so ethical?

Tip 178: Sherry can't write worth a damn'. = Sherry can't write very well at all.
Tip 179: **Win** is the opposite of lose. **Won** is the past form of win.

241. demand /də.mænd/ n.

Other forms: **demand** /də.mænd/ v. **demanding** /də.mæn.dɪŋ/ adj.
Opposite: ask
Meaning: When we demand that someone do something, we insist that they do it. We are ordering them to do it.

Example:
Miss America demanded that I kiss her. She ordered me to do it. I had no choice.

Example:
The collection agency demanded that Jack pay the money he owed on his car and threatened to repossess it if he didn't make the payment in three days.

Tip 180: **repossess** = take it back

242. humanity /hyu.mæn.ə.ti/ n.

Other forms: **human** /hyu.mən/ n.
Meaning: That's all of us, folks.

Example:
The easiest way to doom humanity is to pamper the rich by starving the poor.

243. to perfect /pər.fɛkt/ v.

Other forms: **perfect** /pər.fɛkt/ adj. **perfectionist** /pər.fɛk.shən.ɪst/ n.
Opposite: screw up, foul up
Meaning: To perfect means to make perfect.

Example:
Don was able to perfect his breast stroke in time for the swimming meet.

Example:
Sally is a perfectionist. Everything she does has to be absolutely perfect. She drives her husband nuts!

Tip 181: **nuts** = crazy

244. On the one hand...on the other hand Rel.

Meaning: This expression establishes a contrast between two things or groups of things.

Example:
On the one hand, he's handsome and rich; on the other hand, he's not very honest, so I don't think I'll date him anymore.

Tip 182: **date** = go out with = go on dates with

245. misanthrope /mɪs.æn.θrop/ n.

Other forms: misanthropic /mɪs.ən.θra.pɪk/ adj.
Opposite: humanitarian
Meaning: A misanthrope is a person who hates people.

Example:
Jack hates kids. He hates teenagers. He hates old people. He hates people on welfare. He hates rich people. He hates politicians. He hates lawyers. He hates cops. Come to think of it, I can't think of anyone Jack likes. He must be a misanthrope.

Example:
I think my high school English teacher was a misanthrope.

246. grow /gro/ v.

Other forms: **growth** /groθ/ n.
Opposite: decline
Meaning: The most common meaning of grow is to get bigger, but to grow sometimes means *to become*.

Example:
Stanley grew rich as the years passed.

Example:
As we grow old, our eyesight begins to fail, our hearing fades, our hair begins to thin, our muscles atrophy. Ugh, who wants to grow old?

Paul made a fortune developing computer games.

Practice 84 : Stress test

Directions : Underline the loudest syllable.

1. bluntly 2. dishonest 3. photographer 4. obsessed 5. fortune 6. conflicting 7. inevitable 8. eventual 9. infinite 10. unethical 11. demand 11. humanity 11. perfect 11. misanthrope

Practice 85 : Stickers

Directions : Write a sticker from a story or example in the book that will help you remember what each word means. Cross out the words you already know and concentrate on those you don't.

Example: death & taxes: <u>inevitable</u>

1. to put it bluntly : _____
2. dishonest : _____
3. to tell the truth : _____
4. beat around the bush : _____
5. photographer : _____
6. beak: _____
7. monk : _____
8. obsessed : _____
9. make a fortune : _____
10. conflicting views : _____
11. inevitable : _____
12. eventual : _____
13. infinite : _____
14. unethical : _____
15. demand : _____
16. humanity : _____
17. perfect : _____
18. on the one hand : _____
19. misanthrope : _____
20. grow : _____

Practice 86 : Using Your Own Experience

Directions: Write your own "story" and sticker to help you remember these words. If you already know a word, you don't need a sticker, of course, so write stories or examples only for those words you have trouble with.

1. to put it bluntly :
---

2. dishonest :
---

3. to tell the truth :
---

4. beat around the bush :
---

5. photographer :
---

6. beak :
---

7. monk :
---

8. obsessed :
---

9. make a fortune :
---

10. conflicting views :
---

11. inevitable :
---

12. eventual :
---

13. infinite :
---

14. unethical :

---

15. demand :
_____
_____
16. humanity :
_____
_____
17. perfect :
_____
_____
18. on the one hand :
_____
_____
19. misanthrope :
_____
_____
20. grow :
_____
_____

This guy's got quite a beak.

Practice 87 : Simple Connections

Directions : Choose a word that <u>suggests</u> the meaning of the boldfaced word. Put the appropriate letter in the blank.

a. direct **b.** lie **c.** honest **d.** indirect **e.** camera **f.** mouth **g.** spiritual **h.** focused **i.** rich **j.** disagree **k.** guaranteed **l.** sooner or later **m.** no end **n.** dishonest **o.** insist **p.** us **q.** make 100% OK **r.** contrast **s.** hates people **t.** become

1. Ted is an amateur **photographer**. __
2. **To tell the truth**, Harry is a bit dishonest. __
3. On the other hand, the **monk** is quite honest. __
4. Bill and Gary had **conflicting views** until they ran out of conversation. __
5. Gloria stormed out of the room because she believed company officials were supporting a **dishonest** marketing plan. __
6. Frances was **unethical** only in small ways, for example when she spent $500 on clothes and told her husband she spent only *a little* over $100. __
7. For us finite beings, death is **inevitable**. __
8. **On the one hand**, the job applicant had the necessary educational background. On the other, he didn't have any experience. __
9. The day **grew** cool as the clouds gradually filtered out the sunlight. __
10. Some days seem **infinite**. __
11. After George screwed up the account, the boss **demanded** to see his brains. __
12. The Devil **made a fortune** selling wood burning stoves. __
13. ---
    Sue: The cat's up in the tree.
    Bob : Don't worry about it. **Eventually**, it'll come down. __
14. They worked all night trying to **perfect** the approach they had decided to use with the new client. __
15. **To put it bluntly**, it wasn't perfect in the morning. __
16. Larry worked especially hard at not being a **misanthrope** after Katy divorced him and her family accused him of breaking up their marriage. __
17. ---
    Sarah: Stop **beating around the bush** and tell me what he looks like. __
18. ---
    Cindy: OK, to begin with, his nose looks like a **beak**.
    Sarah : You're kidding!
    Cindy: Would I lie? __
19. Charlie is **obsessed** with the stock market. That's all he ever talks about. __
20. A misanthrope hates **humanity**, including himself, we assume. __

Practice 88 : Similarities

Directions: Write a word in each blank which has a meaning similar to the words given.

1. date : _____ _____
2. in the long run : _____ _____ _____

Practice 89 : Opposites

Directions: Choose a word that means the opposite of the boldfaced word. Put the appropriate letter in the blank.

a. tactful **b.** get to the point **c.** disinterested
d. compatible **e.** won't happen **f.** finite **g.** honest
h. ask **i.** screw up **j.** humanitarian

1. Stop **beating around the bush** and give me your example of a paradox. __
2. The prince, who was used to getting his way, **demanded** that Shirley love him. __
3. It was **inevitable** that Harvey would lose all his money in Las Vegas. You see, he was convinced that he was a good poker player. __
4. **To put it bluntly**, Uncle Stanley isn't very nice. __
5. Nevertheless, he isn't a **misanthrope**. __
6. Shirley and the prince had **conflicting views** about love. __
7. Fred was **obsessed** with the mysterious hole in the ground. __
8. The scientists attempted to **perfect** the thermal tiles on the space craft. __
9. Some school board members were **unethical**. They helped businesses get a better deal from the district. Later, those businesses contributed to the board members' re-election campaigns. __
10. Sandy seems to have an **infinite** number of friends. __

Practice 90: Do these make sense, or not?

Directions: If the information in the sentence is consistent, if everything fits OK, if there are no contradictions, nothing improbable or impossible, then write YES in the blank. However, if the parts don't fit, if it doesn't make sense, if its ridiculous or absurd, then write NO in the blank.

1. One politician to another : It's simply **unethical** of you to tell the truth! __
2. To tell the truth, Bill didn't understand why the **photographer** took his photograph until the photo ended up in the Worst Dressed Citizen Award story in the local newspaper. __
3. Harold **grew** his relationship with his boss until it paid off with a promotion. __
4. **Misanthropes** can be frightening. __
5. Tom never thinks things through. With him, jumping to conclusions is **inevitable.** __
6. **To tell the truth,** Henry was dishonest when he reported the data in the study. __
7. There are times when **humanity** is not very human. __
8. The land development was an **obsession** for Miguel, but he really didn't have the time to give it much attention. __
9. **To put it bluntly**, I think it's in the realm of possibility that you could consider re-evaluating your position on this matter. __
10. Mike has an **infinite** number of jokes. __
11. A monk is basically **dishonest**. __
12. Eventually, you're going to find a grain of truth in what she says, but it'll take you a while because she **beats around the bush** so much.__
13. Lee Teng-Hui and leaders of the PRC had **conflicting views** about the status of Taiwan. __
14. Get your **beak** out of my diary! I told you it was personal! __
15. Shirley thought, "On **the one hand**, he isn't very handsome. On the other hand, he is funny and interesting. __
16. Ed **made a fortune** by relaxing around the house on weekends. __
17. In the early morning, there was lots of **demand** for vegetables at the market. __
18. Pamela **perfected** her wardrobe by purchasing a $40,000 mink coat. __
19. **Eventually**, Carol's curiosity will be rewarded. __

Really?

<u>Directions</u>: Explain your answers to these items :

3. _____
4. _____
9. _____
14. _____
16. _____
13. _____
15. _____

Write

<u>Directions</u>: Write a sentence of your own for each of the words you are learning. Do not write sentences for words you already know. Instead, write a sentence for any substitute words you have chosen to learn.

Lesson 13 Study Guide

Word	Substitute	Similar	Opposite	Memory	✓
to put it bluntly					
dishonest					
to tell the truth					
to beat around the bush					
photographer					
beak					
monk					
obsessed					
to make a fortune					
conflicting views					
inevitable					
eventual					
infinite					
unethical					
demand					
humanity					
to perfect					
on the one hand					
on the other hand					
misanthrope					

Lesson 14 Focus Sheet

Word	✓	Subst Word	Listen	Speak	Read	Write
point of view						
meaningless						
miserable						
furious						
disturbing						
actor						
gesture						
genetics						
puppet						
interpret						
circumstances						
to settle for less						
to cry over spilled milk						
expectation						
in a rut						
confined						
cynic						
cowardice						
distrust						
failure						
to give comfort to someone						

Lesson 14

247. point of view /point əv vyu/ n.

Meaning: Our point of view is the way we see things, the way we look at things, the positions we take. It is often used to mean someone's opinion.

Example:
Bill: What do you think of Charley?
Marion: You might like him, but from my point of view he's a bore. He's one of the most boring men I've ever met.

248. meaningless /mi.nɪŋ.ləs/ adj.

Other forms: **meaning** /mi.nɪŋ/ n.
Opposite: meaningful
Meaning: If something is meaningless, it has no meaning.

Example:
Some people think life is meaningless.

Example:
Hal was tired of going out with a lot of different women. He wanted a meaningful relationship with one woman.

249. miserable /mɪ.zər.ə.bəl/ adj.

Other forms: **misery** /mɪ.zər.i/ n.
Opposite: happy
Meaning: When someone is miserable, he or she is very unhappy. Misery = unhappiness.

Example:
Robin was miserable. She hated her job. She hated her apartment. She also didn't like her boyfriend much.

Example:
Misery loves company. (When people are miserable, they want you to be miserable too.)

250. furious /fyʊr.i.əs/ adj.

Other forms: **fury** /fyʊr.i/ n.
Opposite: calm
Meaning: A furious person is very, very angry.

Example:
Helen was furious when she saw that someone had hit her car in the parking lot while she was in the store. She was particularly furious that the bastard had driven away without leaving a note or anything. (**bastard** = a child born to parents who are not married)

Example:
There was tremendous damage from the storm's fury.

251. disturbing /dɪs.tər.bɪŋ/ adj.

Other forms: **disturb** /dɪs.tərb/ v. **disturbance** /dɪs.tər.bəns/ n.
Opposite (of disturb): leave alone, don't bother
Meaning: If you disturb people, you bother them, you upset them. If something is disturbing, it bothers you or worries you; it troubles you.

Example:
The news about the senseless killing in Bosnia was very disturbing.

Example:
There was a disturbance at the graduation party. Some people were drunk and they got into a fight, so the cops came and told everybody to go home.

Tip 183: **cops** = police.

252. actor /æk.tər/ n.

Other forms: **actress** /æk.trəs/ n. **act** /ækt/ n./v.
Meaning: An actor is a male who plays a role in a play, a movie, a TV show, etc. An actress is a female who does that.

Example:
The actor stepped on stage, said the line, "Darling, I love you," then tripped and fell on his face. It was not the tender love scene the director had hoped it would be.

Example:
The actress created a character that was quite believable..

Tip 184: **quite** = very
Tip 185: **tender** = warm, loving

253. gesture /jɛs.chʊr/ n.

Other forms: **gesture** /jɛs.chʊr/ v.
Opposite: give no sign, make no movement
Meaning: A gesture is a movement of the body (including facial expressions) which conveys a message to an observer.

Example:
The gesture people make when they want to ask (without saying anything necessarily) "Do you mean me?" differs among cultures. In the US people point to their chests. In other places, people point to their chins or to their noses. Same meaning, different gesture.

Example:
George looked across the room and saw the amazingly beautiful woman looking at him. He could not keep his eyes off her. When she winked at him, he got up and went over to her table and sat down. She was obviously bothered by that and she told him to leave. Surprised, George said, "You winked. I thought you wanted me to come over." The woman looked at him and said coldly, "I didn't wink. I blinked. "

Tip 186: **convey** = send
Tip 187: **without saying anything necessarily** = It isn't necessary to say something, but people do sometimes.
Tip 188: **amazingly beautiful** = very, very beautiful
Tip 189: **wink** = close and open one eye
Tip 190: **blink** = close and open both eyes at the same time

254. genetics /jə.nɛ.dɪks/ n.

Other forms: **genes** /jinz/ n. **genetic** /jə.nɛ.dɪk/ adj.
Opposite: incomprehensible
Meaning: Genetics is the study of heredity and the evolution of and behavior of characteristics or traits in living organisms. How's that for a definition? Geneticists trace characteristics passed down from one generation to future generations.

Example:
Harry is hairy, very hairy. He obviously has a lot of hairy genes in his genetic makeup.

Example:
The study of genetics has spawned the biotech industry which is, for example, spawning fish that are twice the size of any of its kind now found in the ocean.

Tip 191: **heredity** = the transmission of traits or characteristics from parent to child
Tip 192: **spawn** = give birth to (most often used for the birth of fish)

255. puppet /pə.pɪt/ n.

Other forms: **puppeteer** /pə.pə.**tir**/ n.
Meaning: A puppet is a doll of some kind that is controlled by a puppeteer who pulls strings attached to the puppet to make the puppet move in this way or that. The more general meaning of puppet is anyone who is completely controlled by someone else.

Example:
Jack thinks we are all puppets, controlled by fate. He believes that our lives are all predetermined and that we just act out our roles without having any control over our lives.

Example:
I can see why Jack believes that. His wife controls him as if he were a puppet.

Tip 193: **fate** = a predetermined conclusion

256. interpret /ɪn.tər.prət/ v.

Other forms: **interpretation** /ɪn.tər.prət.**te**.shən/ n.
Meaning: To interpret means to (1) define or (2) explain from a particular point of view.

Example:
The playwright's directions for playing the character were difficult to interpret. Marge had to interpret the role based on what she thought the writer wanted the character to be like.

Example:
I don't like his poetry because it just takes too much work to interpret what he's getting at.

Tip 194: **what he's getting at** = what he means

257. circumstances /sər.kəm.stæn.səs/ n. (plural)

Other forms: **circumstantial** /sər.kəm.**stæn**.shəl/ adj.
Opposite: not dependent on time and place or conditions
Meaning: When we say something depends on the circumstances, we mean that it depends on the situation, the surroundings, the conditions, the environment, the atmosphere in which it takes place.

Example:
Marty was going to tell his wife that he wanted to change jobs, but he didn't because the circumstances were not right. His wife was still upset about their checking account being overdrawn because he had bought a new set of golf clubs.

Example:
That is a lousy plan under the best circumstances. You can imagine how much harm it will do under less than ideal circumstances.

Tip 195: **to imagine** = to guess, to picture

258. to settle for less /sɛ.dəl for lɛs/ Idiom

Other forms: **settle** /sɛ.dəl/ v. **settlement** /sɛ.dəl.mənt/
Opposite: get more than you thought you would get
Meaning: If you settle for less, you take less than you could get.

Example:
Sam wanted to sell his car for around $3,000, but the best offer he got was $2,200 so he had to settle for less.

Example:
Don't settle for less in life. Work hard. Try hard. Be smart. Make the best of circumstances. Identify your dream and go for it!

259. to cry over spilled milk /spɪld/ Idiom

Opposite: accept what has happened
Meaning: A person who cries over spilled milk complains about something after it has already happened and nothing can be done.

Example:
John was always crying over spilled milk. He had good reason to. When he was in the Navy during World War II he met an old woman in Florida who liked him very much. One day she told him that she wanted to sell her property. She said she wanted to sell it to him because she knew he would take good care of it. The price was very low, but John didn't have enough money to buy it. The lady told him that he could make payments, only $35 a month, until he could save enough money to pay it off completely. John thought about buying the property, but decided not to because he was being transferred to Guam in a month and he didn't know where the Navy would send him next.

On a September morning two years after the war had ended, John was reading the newspaper when he saw a story about the DuPont family buying property in Florida for their new home. The DuPonts, who owned the DuPont Chemical Corporation, were millionaires and the house they would build would be worth millions of dollars. As John read, he learned that the DuPont's house would be built right across the road from the property the old lady had offered him for $35 a month. He realized then, of course, that if he had bought the old lady's property, he would be a millionaire himself. Ever since that day, John complained about not buying the old lady's property. Whenever he thought of it, he would say, "I could kick myself for not buying that land."

Example:
John had another reason for crying over spilled milk. After the war in 1948, John's brother-in-law, Paul, came over to the house one day and told him about 1,000 acres in Poway, near San Diego. It was only $200 an acre. Paul wanted to buy it, but he didn't have enough money and he couldn't borrow that much. So he asked John if he would go in on the land with him. John had some money saved and, together, they could have gotten a loan for the rest, but John decided not to do it. That land in Poway is now filled with expensive homes. If John and Paul had bought that land in 1948, they would both be millionaires today. John kicks himself twice a day, once for Florida and once for Poway.

Tip 196: **property** = land and any buildings on it

260 expectation /ɛk.spɛk.te.shən/ n.

Other forms: **expect** /ɛk.spɛkt/ v. (-ed/-ing adj)
Opposite: no expectations, no assumptions about the future
Meaning: If you expect something to happen, you assume it is going to happen, you really believe it is going to happen. That's your expectation.

Example:
Marty had high expectations for his two-year-old son. He hoped his son would become a doctor or a lawyer or a scientist or an engineer.

Example:
Marty's son became an actor. Sometimes it just isn't a good idea to have expectations.

261. in a rut /rət/ Idiom

Opposite: making progress, getting somewhere
Meaning: If you're in a rut, you're stuck. You can't get anywhere. You don't seem to be able to make any progress at all.

Example:
We're really in a rut. Business has been flat for three months now, and there are no signs that it's going to get any better in the near future.

Example:
I feel like I'm in a rut. I haven't had any good ideas for I don't know how long.

Tip 197: **flat** = stay about the same
Tip 198: **near future** = soon
Tip 199: **for I don't know how long** = for a long time

262. confined /kən.faɪnd/ adj.

Other forms: **confine** /kən.faɪn/ v. **confinement** /kən.faɪn.mənt/ adj.
Opposite: free
Meaning: Confined means being restricted or restrained in some way. A person who is confined is not free to do what he or she wants and, in fact, is prevented from doing so.

Example:
Tommy was confined to his room for lying to his Dad. He had to stay in his room all day until dinner time.

Example:
His public criticism of the mayor was confined to a few remarks at a party, but you should hear what he said to his wife about the mayor!

Tip 200: **remarks** = what he said

263. cynic /sɪn.ɪk/ n.

Other forms: **cynicism** /sɪn.ə.sɪ.zəm/ n. **cynical** /sɪn.ə.kʊl/ adj.
Opposite: a person who is trusting and believing
Meaning: A cynic is a skeptic, a person who doesn't believe that something is true, that something can be done. A cynic's first impulse is to doubt that something is true or possible.

Example:
A cynic distrusts people's motives and tends to assume self-interest in any decision.

Example:
Tom: The only reason the Senator is supporting this legislation is because someone is paying him under the table to do it.
Theresa: Tom don't be so cynical. I believe he's supporting it because it's good for the people in his district.

Tip 201: **self-interest** = doing something to benefit one's self
Tip 202: **under the table** = secretly

264. cowardice /kaʊ.ər.dɪs/ adj.

Other forms: **coward** /kaʊ.ərd/ n.
Opposite: bravery
Meaning: A coward is unwilling to do something that should be done or could be done because he or she is afraid. Informally, we call a coward a chicken. Someone is *chicken* if they are afraid to do something. But people are not chickens all over the world: In Vietnam a coward is a rabbit. In Japan a coward is a kind of bug. Cowards morph into various other creatures in other parts of the world.

Example:
A cynic would say that all politicians are cowards. The cynic says they are afraid to do what's right because they are scared they will lose votes in the next election.

Example:
Cowardice has saved more than a few lives - the lives of the cowards, of course. The coward's motto is, "When in doubt, run!"

Tip 203: **morph** (adj. = metamorphic) = become transformed into a different creature (or whatever)

265. distrust /dɪs.trəst/ v.

Other forms: **distrustful** /dɪs.trəst.fʊl/ adj. **distrusting** /dɪs.trəst.ɪŋ/ adj.
Opposite: trust
Meaning: If you distrust someone, you don't trust him, of course.

Example:
Distrust has damaged and destroyed many relationships.

Example:
Helen: I think she distrusts him.
Jamie: Why?
Helen: I overheard her telling him, "I trust you as far as I can throw you."

266. failure /fel.yər/ n.

Other forms: **fail** /fel.əl/ v. **failing** /fe.lɪŋ/ adj.
Opposite: success
Meaning: If you fail, you don't make it, you don't succeed. If you failed to do something, you didn't do it.

Example:
Frank failed to get the contact, but his failure didn't stop him. He got three other contracts the following week. Frank's attitude is, "Failure makes me work harder to succeed."

Example:
His failure to inform the boss that the project would be delayed another three weeks led to his dismissal. In other words, he was canned for not telling the boss that the project would be completed late.

Tip 204: **16 ways to get fired** = He was: dismissed, canned, dumped, let go, discharged, removed, ousted, booted out, forced out, drummed out, surplused, bounced, given a pink slip, given his walking papers, given the bum's rush, and given the old heave-ho.

267. give comfort to someone /kəm.fərt/ Idiom

Other forms: **comfort** /kəm.fərt/ v/n. **comfortable** /kəm.fər.də.bəl/ adj.
Opposite: disturb or distress someone
Meaning: If you give comfort to someone, you help them feel better after something not so good has happened, i.e. you comfort that person.

Example:
The large bonus he received at work gave him comfort. It comforted him. It made him feel a lot more comfortable as he looked at the credit card bills.

Example:
We are not comforted by victory when so many lives have been lost.

Jack is really the puppet.

Practice 91 : Stress test

Directions : Underline the loudest syllable.

1. meaningless 2. miserable 3. furious 4. disturb
5. actor 6. gesture 7. genetics 8. puppet 9. interpret
10. circumstances 11. expectation 12. continued 13. cynic
14. cowardice 15. distrust 16. failure 17. comfort

Practice 92 : Stickers

Directions : Write a sticker from a story or example in the book that will help you remember what each word means. Cross out the words you already know and concentrate on those you don't.

Example: coward : When in doubt, run!

1. point of view : _____
2. meaningless : _____
3. miserable : _____
4. furious : _____
5. disturb : _____
6. actor : _____
7. gesture : _____
8. genetics : _____
9. puppet : _____
10. interpret : _____
11. circumstances : _____
12. settle for less : _____
13. cry over spilt milk : _____
14. expectation : _____
15. in a rut : _____
16. confined : _____
17. cynic : _____
18. cowardice : _____
19. distrust: _____
20. failure : _____
21. give comfort to : _____

Practice 93 : Using Your Own Experience

Directions : Write your own "story" and sticker to help you remember these words. If you already know a word, you don't need a sticker, of course, so write stories or examples only for those words you have trouble with.

1. point of view :
_____
_____
2. meaningless :
_____
_____
3. miserable :
_____
_____
4. furious :
_____
_____
5. disturb :
_____
_____
6. actor :
_____
_____
7. gesture :
_____
_____
8. genetics :
_____
_____
9. puppet :
_____
_____
10. interpret :
_____
_____
11. circumstances :
_____
_____
12. settle for less :
_____
_____
13. cry over split milk :
_____
_____
14. expectation :
_____
_____

15. in a rut :
_____
_____

16. confined :
_____
_____

17. cynic :
_____
_____

18. cowardice :
_____
_____

19. distrust :
_____
_____

20. failure :
_____
_____

21. give comfort to :
_____
_____

Practice 94 : Simple Connections

Directions : Choose a word that <u>suggests</u> the meaning of the boldfaced word. Put the appropriate letter in the blank.

a. position **b.** without meaning **c.** very unhappy **d.** very angry
e. bother **f.** performer **g.** movement **h.** heredity **i.** controlled **j.** explain
k. dependent **l.** didn't get as much as was possible **m.** complain
n. assume **o.** stuck **p.** restricted **q.** skeptic **r.** chicken **s.** watch 'em!
t. didn't make it **u.** feel better

1. Under the **circumstances**, I wouldn't lend you a dime. __
2. John **gestured** for Mary to come over to his desk. __
3. Dave has been **in a rut** for quite some time. He hasn't been able to accomplish anything lately. __
4. From Sally's **point of view**, Sharon was a jerk. __
5. Sandy's promises are **meaningless** because she never delivers what she promises. __
6. The dog that frightened everyone was filled with instant **cowardice** when it faced the tiger. __
7. Sam **distrusts** people who smile too much. __
8. We were **disturbed** in the middle of the night by the tree that fell through the roof of our house and landed at the foot of our bed. __
9. Gloria was **furious** that her secretary had left the office three hours early without telling her. __
10. Fred believes that admitting his mistakes **gives comfort to** those who want his job, so he never does. __
11. "I'm an **actress**, not a puppet," Candy screamed as she stormed off the stage. __
12. The King had no real power. He was just a **puppet** of those who really controlled the country. __
13. ---
    <u>Gary</u>: How are you feeling, Karen? You don't look too good.
    <u>Karen</u>: I'm **miserable**. I've got the flu, bad. __
14. Mike received the following note from his supervisor: "Your **failure** to work overtime has cost you a promotion." Mike sued the supervisor and the company for unfair labor practices and won. He is now the supervisor's boss. __
15. Susan was **confined** to a wheelchair for three months after the accident. __
16. Ed was in a hurry to sell his car, so he **settled for less** than he could have gotten if he had waited for his price. __
17. ---
    <u>Sarah</u>: Did you hear that Gil and Madge got divorced?
    <u>Cindy</u>: What's so surprising. Marriage is a dead institution.
    <u>Sarah</u> : Don't be so **cynical**, Cindy. There are lots of happily married couples. __
18. Who said **genetics** is fair? I love basketball and my brother Dennis doesn't, but he got all the tall genes and I got all the short ones. __

19. **Don't cry over spilt milk**. The game's over. Second place isn't that bad. Besides, there's always next year. __

20. The courts **interpret** the law. The police enforce the law. __

21. Sam left two hours before flight time, so he **expected** to arrive at the airport in plenty of time to catch the plane to Hong Kong, but he got caught in the traffic from the eight car pileup on the freeway and missed his flight. __

Practice 95 : Similarities

Directions : Write a word in each blank which has a meaning similar to the words given.

1. expect : _____ _____
2. in a rut : _____ _____ _____
3. disturbing : _____ _____ _____
4. get fired : _____ _____ _____ _____ _____ _____ _____ _____ _____ _____ _____ _____ _____ _____ _____ _____

Practice 96 : Opposites

Directions : Choose a word that means the opposite of the boldfaced word. Put the appropriate letter in the blank.

a. meaningful b. happy c. calm
d. leave alone e. get more f. It won't happen. g. progress
h. free i. bravery j. success

1. I know, you're **miserable** because you can't think of a paradox. __
2. Paul felt **confined** in that office job, so he quit and got a job as a garbage man. Now, he's dirty, but he's free. __
3. It was his **expectation** that he would be a millionaire by the time he was thirty-five, but he was a failure. He didn't become a millionaire until he was thirty-six. __
4. Dan thought life was **meaningless** until he met Jane. __
5. The sign on the hotel room door said, "Do not **disturb**." I wonder what they're doing in there. __
6. Part of the letter from the IRS read : "Your **failure** to pay $4,670 for the 1996 taxable year has resulted in penalties of $6730. Please submit the total of $11,400 in ten days. __
7. Of course, Pat was **furious** when she received that letter from the IRS because she had already paid her 1996 taxes in full. __
8. Ken's bravery was only exceeded by his **cowardice**. __
9. Mary could have married Tex, who was rich and handsome, but she **settled for** Fred, who was only rich, because she couldn't stand Tex's mother. __
10. I'm **in a rut**. I can't think of an interesting example for this one. __

Practice 97: Do these make sense, or not?

Directions: If the information in the sentence is consistent, if everything fits OK, if there are no contradictions, nothing improbable or impossible, then write YES in the blank. However, if the parts don't fit, if it doesn't make sense, if its ridiculous or absurd, then write NO in the blank.

1. Trying to think of paradoxes can make one **miserable**. __
2. Bill stuck him with his **point of view**. __
3. Harold's telling me that he would pay me back double if I lent him $1,000 was **meaningless** since he never repaid his debts. __
4. Rock singers are the result of faulty **genetics**. __
5. Everything had gone just the way he planned, so naturally he was **furious**. __
6. Claire was **crying over spilt milk** after she won the lottery. __
7. The **cynic** thought that you could make it if you really tried. __
8. It was blistering hot that day, and Marvin got a terrible sunburn because he **failed** to bring his sun block. __
9. The actor felt **confined** by the Director's continual instructions. __
10. The report was somewhat nebulous so we had some trouble **interpreting** it. __
11. The actor was **disturbed** by the burping in the audience. __
12. If you want to learn how to be a **coward** imitate an astronaut. __
13. Maria **comforted** Juan after he won the race. __
14. That particular **gesture** - extending the arm and raising the middle finger in another's face - is designed to produce a fight. __
15. Harry wanted to go to Stanford, but he couldn't afford it, so he **settled for** San Jose State University - less prestige, but affordable. __
16. We're **in a rut**. Let's go out of town and get a change of scenery. __
17. **Puppets** can be independent little creatures. __
18. They were sitting there in the little French restaurant having a candlelight dinner as the violinist played in the background. Harvey really wanted to ask Carol to marry him, but the **circumstances** were just not right. __
19. After three years of "We'll get married pretty soon," Carol was beginning to distrust Harvey. __
20. Gertrude **expected** to be out of town for a while, so she stopped the paper and asked a neighbor to feed the cat. __

Really?
Directions: Explain your answers to these items:

2. _____
4. _____
18. _____

Write

Directions: Write a sentence of your own for each of the words you are learning. Do not write sentences for words you already know. Instead, write a sentence for any substitute words you have chosen to learn.

Lesson 14 Study Guide

Word	Substitute	Similar	Opposite	Memory	✓
point of view					
meaningless					
miserable					
furious					
disturbing					
actor					
gesture					
genetics					
puppet					
interpret					
circumstances					
to settle for less					
to cry over spilled milk					
expectation					
in a rut					
confined					
cynic					
cowardice					
distrust					
failure					
to give comfort to someone					

Paul is dirty, but he's free.

Lesson 15 Focus Sheet

Word	✓	Subst Word	Listen	Speak	Read	Write
criticize						
a mess						
constructive						
moan						
whine						
dark visions						
fascinating						
attachment						
wander						
at the drop of a hat						
realism						
stage						
creep						
snail						
oath						
amusing						
jealousy						
ambition						
coarse						
fierce						
intimidate						

Lesson 15

268. criticize /krɪ.də.saiz/ v.

Other forms: **criticisms** /krɪ.də.sɪ.zəm/ n. **critical** /krɪ.də.kəl/ adj.
Opposite: praise
Meaning: Criticize usually has a negative meaning in everyday use. When we criticize something, we point out that there is something wrong with it. We question it.

Example:
James was very critical of his wife. He criticized the way she did just about everything. He told her that she didn't do the dishes right, that she didn't know how to clean the house, that she did a lousy job with the gardening, that her way of emptying the garbage was inefficient, and that she always left marks on the windows when she washed them, for example.

Example:
Because of James's constant criticism, his wife left him. Now James has to do the dishes, clean the house, do the gardening, empty the garbage, wash the windows...

269. a mess /mɛs/ n.

Other forms: **messy** /mɛs.i/ adj. **messiness** /mɛs.i.nəs/ n.
Opposite: neat
Meaning: If something is a mess, it is disorganized, untidy, cluttered, and perhaps confusing. Nothing is in order when there is a mess.

Example:
My son Eben's room was always a mess. When I asked him why he didn't clean it up, he replied that his room was a form of self-expression. He was just expressing his personality, he said. Unfortunately, he was not aware of the significance of his remark.

Example:
The company's marketing plan was a mess, so they hired a marketing consultant to help them develop a better one.

Tip 205: **the significance of his remark** = the meaning of what he said

270. constructive /kən.strək.tɪv/ adj.

Other forms: **construct** /kən.strəkt/ v.
Opposite: destructive
Meaning: To construct means to build. Something that is constructive helps to make something better.

Example:
Marsha criticized the plan, but her criticism was constructive. She pointed out what she thought was wrong with the plan, but she also suggested ways to improve it.

Example:
Constructive criticism provides hope for a solution. Destructive criticism provides a vacuum.

Tip 206: vacuum = nothingness = emptiness = a void

271. moan /mon/ v.

Other forms: **moaning** /mo.nɪŋ/ n/adj.
Meaning: Moaning is a sound made when someone is in pain. We moan when we are in intense pain.

Example:
In the white room with the white curtains in the window and around her bed, she moaned. She had been in labor for three hours. Her black baby did not want to come out.

Example:
Nelson sat on the ground moaning. The heavy carpenter's hammer had fallen from the top of the stepladder onto his big toe.

272. whine /wain/ v.

Other forms: **whine** /wain/ n. **whining** /wai.nɪŋ/ adj.
Meaning: Whining is a complaining tone of voice. It's like crying without tears. Little children whine a lot when they don't get what they want. Adults are not supposed to whine - it's considered childlike behavior - but they sometimes do.

Example:
Her four year old son was whining and kicking as they stood in line waiting to pay for their groceries because he wanted a candy bar and his mom would not buy one for him. The other people in line wanted to put him over their knee and spank his little bottom.

Example:
Rose: Lazy Lorraine is whining again about having too much work to do.
Wilma: You mean she's got to do something besides do her nails and check her mascara?
Rose: Yeah, I'm afraid so. She actually has to do some word processing this afternoon. Can you believe it?
Wilma: Oh my God, she'll be whining about that for two days!

Tip 207: his **bottom** = his butt
Tip 208: **mascara** = a cosmetic (make up) used to darken the eyelashes

273. dark visions /vɪ.ʒənz/ Noun phrase

Other forms: **envision** /ɛn.vɪ.ʒən/ v.
Opposite: bright outlook for the future
Meaning: In this phrase dark means terrible. Envision means to imagine something that could happen in the future. One's vision refers to what one imagines the future will be like.

Example:
Allen has a dark vision of the future. He thinks continued air pollution will destroy the ozone layer which protects us from the sun's heat and radioactivity, and we will all fry (sunny side up, of course).

Example:
Allen's wife envisions a brighter future for us. She sees everyone driving solar powered cars with solar panels on their roofs. These cars will not emit pollutants, helping to preserve the ozone layer and prevent us from being in the frying pan, as she puts it.

Tip 209: **to imagine** = to picture = to conceive = to suppose = to conjecture = to guess
Tip 210: air **pollution** = anything which dirties the air, making it hard for us to breathe, producing lung cancer, etc.
Tip 211: **envision** = verb form of vision
Tip 212: **emit** = send out.

274. fascinating /fæ.sɪn.e.dɪŋ/ adj.

Other forms: **fascinate** /fæ.sɪn.et/ v. **fascination** /fæ.sɪn.e.shən/ n.
Opposite: dull, uninteresting
Meaning: Fascinating means very interesting.

Example:
Zelda is a fascinating person. She's an artist who loves to go deep sea diving and play poker. She's an expert on Amazon medicines, and has written many books about them, and she is building her own house on an island near Vancouver all by herself. (Is that fascinating enough for ya?)

Example:
Pat: Dave is fascinated by his Koi. He could watch them swimming around in the pond all day long.
Nick: I know. He's knows every one of them by name.
Pat: By name?
Nick: Yeah, he named every one of them. Yesterday I saw him walking over to the garden hose with one of the fish in his pocket. I asked him what he had in his pocket and he said it was Freddie. He told me he was going to give Freddie a bath.

Tip 213: **poker** = a card game

275. attachment /ə.tæch.mənt/ n.

Other forms: **attach** /ə.tæch/ v. **attached** /ə.tæcht/ adj.
Opposite: detached
Meaning: To attach means to connect, so attachment means connection. An object can be attached to another object and people can be attached to each other, i.e. they can have a close relationship with each other.

Example:
The philosopher told us all about how meaningless life is and about how ridiculous people are, but he formed his ideas in a room by himself, never getting out into the real world to see what life and people were really like. He had attachments to no one.

Example:
When I was two years old, my Aunt Pat took me for a walk. When we were on our way back home, I started to cry and I kept saying, "My buggie, my buggie." Aunt Pat didn't know what I was trying to say, so when we arrived at my house she asked my Mom what "buggie" meant. My Mom told her it meant "bunny." That's when my Aunt and my Mom saw what had happened. I was standing there crying and holding only my bunny's ear. When my Aunt Pat and I started out on the walk, the rest of the bunny was attached to the ear. (Happy ending: My Aunt Pat bought me a new bunny the following day.)

Tip 214: **ridiculous** = foolish

276. wander /wan.dər/ v.

Other forms: **wandering** /wan.dər.ɪŋ/ adj
Opposite: head right for a destination, go directly to a place you planned to go to
Meaning: To wander means to walk around without any particular destination, without any particular goal or reason or plan.

Example:
Yolanda wandered around in the woods enjoying the scent of the redwood trees and the flowers and the sounds of the forest creatures, finding an interesting patch here and another there until the air began to chill. Then she returned home - with a relaxing, refreshing afternoon in her pocket.

Example:
After two days, the Alzheimer's patient was found wandering around the old part of town. He didn't know his name. He didn't know where he was. The only thing he said to the police was, "I want pancakes with pure maple syrup from Virginia."

Tip 215: **scent** = smell
Tip 216: **patch** = place with flowers and other vegetation
Tip 217: **chill** = get cold

277. at the drop of a hat /dræp/ Idiom

Opposite: slowly, thoughtfully
Meaning: At the drop of a hat means doing something quickly, immediately, right away without thinking very much about it.

Example:
Rich and I were at UC Berkeley waiting for a seminar to begin the following morning when, at the drop of a hat, he said, "Let's go to Reno and try our luck tonight." I looked at him for a second, nodded my head, and we left. We returned the next morning in time for the first session $430 richer. Sometimes, it pays to do something at the drop of a hat.

278. realism /ri.əl.ɪ.zəm/ n.

Other forms: **reality** /ri.æl.ɪ.ti/ n. **realist** /ri.əl.ɪst/ n. **real** /ri.əl/ adj. **realistic** /ri.əl.lɪs.tɪk/ adj.
Opposite: fantasy
Meaning: Whatever is real is not fake or false. It's genuine. It's the real thing. A realist is someone who tries to see the world the way it really is. When we attempt to see things the way they are, rather than the way we would like them to be, we are being realistic.

Example:
Gary was tired of working with his hands; he wanted a white collar job that paid a lot of money for someone to sit behind a desk. However, he wasn't being very realistic. He didn't have a college degree. He had taken only a couple of courses at a community college. Without a degree, it was unrealistic for him to think that he could get a white collar job.

Example:
Liz wanted ten kids, but she was a realist. She knew she couldn't afford to raise ten children, so she settled for three kids and a bunch of rabbits.

Tip 218: **white collar job** = office job, professional work

279. stage /stej/ n.

Meaning: A play is performed **on** a stage. Singers sing **on** stage. Dancers dance **on** stage.

Example:
After the actor had fallen on his face on stage, his lovely girlfriend walked over to him, put her foot on his back, and said, "This is symbolic of what our relationship will be, darling."

Example:
The dancer turned in the air and promptly fell **off** the stage into the audience. He must be the actor's brother.

280. creep /krip/ v.

Other forms: **crept** /krɛpt/ v. (past) **creeping** /kri.pɪŋ/ adj.
Opposite: run
Meaning: To go slowly, often bending down while one moves to avoid being seen.

Example:
Olga crept into the restaurant without being noticed by anyone. She then crept behind the fake palm trees that separated her from her boyfriend and the woman with whom he was having dinner. She was standing there quietly, listening to her boyfriend telling this woman how much he loved her and wanted her children, when she spotted the large plate of spaghetti.

Example:
Luz crept into the office 45 minutes late, hoping the boss would not see her. As she slipped into the chair at her desk, she breathed a sigh of relief. She still had a perfect record. She had never been late for work in 12 years at the company.

Tip 219: **the woman with whom he was having dinner** = the woman he was having dinner with. **spotted** = saw
Tip 220: **slipped into the chair** = gently sat down
Tip 221: **sigh** = exhale (breathe out) loudly

281. snail /sneəl/ n.

Meaning: A very slow garden creature that lives in a shell.

Example:
He walks to work like a pregnant snail . It's only a month now before he is to be laid off. He doesn't know whether he'll have another job by then.

Example:
My brother Dick and I moved towards school every morning like snails on their way to a funeral. On Mondays, Wednesdays, and Fridays the rule was: You can't step on any line on the sidewalk; if you do, you get punched hard in the arm. On Tuesdays and Thursdays the rule was: You have to step on every line on the sidewalk. If you miss one, you get punched in the arm. We set it up this way because we knew one of us would forget what day it was from time to time. It made it more interesting.

Tip 222: **pregnant** = going to have a baby
Tip 223: **layoff** = a nicer (well, at least milder) word for firing someone

282. oath /oθ/ n.

Meaning: When you swear an oath, you promise that you will do something. You pledge that you will do it. You vow that you will do it.

Example:
One of the most solemn oaths one can take is the marriage vow used in many weddings: "I promise to love and cherish you until death."

Example:
When I was elected a school board member, I had to take an oath to defend my country against all enemies at home and abroad. I don't know why I had to take that oath since a school board member's job is simply to make policies for the school district.

Tip 224: **solemn** = serious
Tip 225: **abroad** = overseas = outside the country

283. amusing /ə.myu.ʒɪŋ/ adj.

Other forms: **amused** /ə.myuʒd/ adj. **amusement** /ə.myuʒ.mənt/ n.
Opposite: not funny
Meaning: If something is amusing, it is mildly humorous. It's funny, but it's not so funny that it has you rolling on the ground.

Example:
Grandpa was amused as he watched his four and five-year-old grandchildren playing in the park.

Example:
Matthew was not amused when he saw his teenage daughter dressed up like Madonna.

284. jealousy /jɛl.ə.si/ n.

Other forms: **jealous** /jɛl.əs/ adj. (-ly adv)
Opposite: trusting
Meaning: When people are jealous, they often are threatened when their lover spends "too much" time with another person or gives another person "too much" attention. A jealous person feels insecure and is afraid to lose the person he or she loves.

Example:
"Jealousy doth mock the meat it feeds on." (Othello) means something like " Jealousy ridicules or disrespects the love that the jealous person is afraid to lose. "

Example:
Mary was jealous of Sam's dog. She thought he spent too much time with the dog and not enough with her and that he cared more for the dog than for her. She even thought Sam gave the dog a better Christmas present than he gave her, even though she doesn't like bones or dog biscuits.

Tip 226: **insecure** = unsafe = vulnerable
Tip 227: **ridicule** = make fun of
Tip 228: **disrespect** have no respect for = treating someone or something like it had little value

285. ambition /æm.bɪ.shən/ n.

Other forms: **ambitious** /æm.bɪ.shəs/ adj. (-ly adv)
Opposite: laziness
Meaning: An ambitious person tries very hard to succeed, to get ahead, to continue to improve his or her position.

Example:
Derrick is definitely an ambitious person. He's now working as a salesman for the company, but he says in five years he is going to be the company president.

Example:
Erik is filled with ambition. He's writing his first book now. He tells himself that he is gong to finish ten books in the next three years.

286. coarse /kors/ adj.

Other forms: **coarseness** /kors.nəs/ n.
Opposite: smooth
Meaning: Coarse means rough, not smooth. A surface can be coarse. Language can be coarse. Sandpaper is coarse.

Example:
Mr. Wilson: How was your exam, Rod?
Rod: Oh it was a real son of a bitch, Mr. Wilson.
Mr. Wilson: Oh... uh...how are you doing in your other classes?
Rod: Oh real shitty because the teachers are all bastards.
Mr. Wilson didn't like Rod because of his coarse language, because he swears a lot.

Example:
When he fell, he scraped his elbow on the coarse surface of the street. It wasn't a serious injury, but it sure looked like it. There was blood everywhere.

Tip 229: **son of a bitch** = son of a female dog
Tip 230: **shitty** = lousy
Tip 231: **bastards** = babies born to parents who are not married
Tip 232: **swear** = to use coarse language

287. fierce /firs/ adj.

Other forms: **fierceness** /firs.nəs/ n. (-ly adv)
Opposite: harmless
Meaning: Anything that is fierce is dangerous, even deadly. Wild animals can be fierce. A military attack can be fierce. The 49er passing attack can be fierce.

Example:
The fierce beast jumped out of the dark night onto the back of the ox. We didn't know what it was until the next day when we saw the black leopard feeding on the carcass.

Example:
The fierce running attack of the Dallas Cowboys (America's team) was stopped cold by the Oakland Raiders (my team).

Tip 233: **beast** = wild animal

288. intimidate /ɪn.tɪm.ə.det/ v.

Other forms: **intimidation** /ɪn.tɪm.ə.de.shən/ v. **intimidating** /ɪn.tɪm.ə.de.dɪŋ/ adj. **intimidated** /ɪn.tɪm.ə.de.dəd/ adj.
Opposite: make someone feel comfortable
Meaning: If someone intimidates you, you feel uncomfortable because you are afraid; you sense danger. You may be apprehensive because of that person's appearance or manner.

Example:
Ralph Lee, the Evening Dean who was 6'8" tall and 280 pounds, certainly intimidated me. One night, he visited one of my classes. After class, Ralph asked me, a 5'7" first year teacher, to see him the following day. When I walked into his office, he was standing by his desk. He looked down at me and said in a deep, loud voice, "Good class Stokes." I looked up at him and squeaked back in the manner of a live chicken being plucked, "Thanks, Ralph."

Example:
A guy named Machiavelli said that intimidation works a lot better than love. Of course, he didn't have many close friends.

Tip 234: **apprehensive** = fearful = nervousness from fear
Tip 235: **manner** = the way someone behaves
Tip 236: **a chicken being plucked** = a chicken having its feathers pulled out

When we started out, I had the whole bunny.

He crept into the room without being noticed.

Practice 98 : Stress test

Directions : Underline the loudest syllable.

1. constructive 2. visions 3. fascinating 4. attachment
5. wander 6. realism 7. amusing 8. jealousy 9. ambition
10. intimidate

Practice 99 : Stickers

Directions : Write a sticker from a story or example in the book that will help you remember what each word means. Cross out the words you already know and concentrate on those you don't.

Example: attachment: <u>Phil's bunny</u>

1. criticize : _____
2. a mess : _____
3. constructive : _____
4. moan : _____
5. whine : _____
6. visions : _____
7. fascinating : _____
8. attachment : _____
9. wander : _____
10. at the drop of a hat : _____
11. realism : _____
12. stage : _____
13. creep : _____
14. snail : _____
15. oath : _____
16. amusing : _____
17. jealousy : _____
18. ambition : _____
19. coarse : _____
20. fierce : _____
21. intimidate : _____

Practice 100 : Using Your Own Experience

Directions: Write your own "story" and sticker to help you remember these words. If you already know a word, you don't need a sticker, of course, so write stories or examples only for those words you have trouble with.

1. messy :
---

2. constructive :
---

3. moan :
---

4. whine :
---

5. visions :
---

6. fascinating :
---

7. attachment :
---

8. wander :
---

9. at the drop of a hat :
---

10. realism :
---

11. stage :
---

12. creep :
---

13. snail :
---

14. oath :
---

15. amusing : _____
_____

16. jealousy : _____
_____

17. ambition : _____
_____

18. coarse : _____
_____

19. fierce : _____
_____

20. intimidate : _____
_____

21. criticize : _____
_____

Practice 101: Simple Connections

Directions: Choose a word that <u>suggests</u> the meaning of the boldfaced word. Put the appropriate letter in the blank.

a. You're wrong. **b.** cluttered **c.** make better **d.** pain **e.** complain
f. terrible **g.** very interesting **h.** connection **i.** no destination **j.** immediately
k. the way it is **l.** performance **m.** slowly **n.** shell **o.** promise **p.** humorous
q. distrust **r.** get ahead **s.** rough **t.** dangerous **u.** threaten

1. Jeremiah's saxophone **moaned** the blues all night. __
2. Joan's belly button was **fascinating**. I've never seen a design like that. __
3. The newspapers **criticized** the judge's handling of the case. __
4. Although the papers thought it was **amusing**, they did not believe it was productive to let a talking dog testify in court. __
5. Some two hours before dawn, a thief **crept** into the darkened studio and stole Ann's painting of a thief stealing a painting from her studio. Can you imagine how the thief felt when he looked at the painting at home? __
6. Victor's **dark visions** of the future were excessive but attention-getting. He always seemed to attract pretty young females who tried to convince him that the future was much brighter than he assumed it would be. __
7. Alice consciously attempted to **intimidate** me, so I let her think she did. Everyone should have a little satisfaction in life. __
8. **Ambition** and brains often accompany one another. Unfortunately, they also intimidate one another. __
9. Hal would lie **at the drop of a hat** if it relieved him of responsibility for an error. __
10. Little Lenny creeps to school every day like a **snail** because he follows a snail to school. __
11. Randy's room and his thinking are a **mess**. __
12. Wanda **wandered** around the shopping mall, killing time in Dallas until her flight home. __
13. ---
    <u>Gary</u>: I left my ticket at home, so they won't let me in. I'm going to sit right here and **whine** until they let me into the dance. __
14. ---
    <u>Nancy</u>: That isn't very **constructive**. Why don't you just drive home and get the ticket? __
15. Susan didn't have a **fierce** bone in her body. __
16. Jan felt secure when he was **jealous**, so she did her best to make him more jealous. That's how she lost him. __
17. ---
    <u>Sarah</u>: Did you hear that Stan and Stella **split up**?
    <u>Cindy</u>: Yeah, I'm wasn't surprised. He was too **attached** to his boat. __

18. The **stage** was filled with dancing girls until the magician made them all disappear. He was fired the next day. __

19. Jim, who had only a high school education, wasn't being very **realistic**. He thought he would get a good-paying job. __

20. When Jeff was elected, he had to take an **oath** that he would defend his country against all enemies. At the time he took the oath, he wondered what kind of weapons they gave out to school board members. __

21. Jake's **coarse** language tended to intimidate others. __

Practice 102: Similarities

Directions: Write a word in each blank which has a meaning similar to the words given.

1. messy : _____ _____ _____
2. vacuum : _____ _____ _____
3. abroad : _____ _____
4. at the drop of a hat : _____ _____ _____
5. imagine : _____ _____ _____ _____ _____

Practice 103 : Opposites

Directions: Choose a word that means the opposite of the boldfaced word. Put the appropriate letter in the blank.

a. praise **b.** destructive **c.** bright outlook
d. detached **e.** thoughtfully **f.** fantasy **g.** dash
h. humorless **i.** laziness **j.** smooth **k.** harmless **l.** make comfortable

1. Some paradoxes are **amusing**. __
2. George, try to be a little more **realistic**. Rosie is not going to go out with you. You're 10 and she's 23, so forget it. __
3. **Ambition** compounded Glen's problems. __
4. Uncle Stanley **criticized** Stan whenever he got the chance. __
5. The tiger looked **fiercely** at the dog and the dog moaned. __
6. Don had no **attachment** to the people he worked with. Every night, he would go home to his own world. __
7. Some of the **dark visions** of the misanthrope are shared by the cynics. __
8. Rich had a **coarse** beard when he was a young man. __
9. Paula's advice was **constructive**. She told Todd that, even though it would work, killing himself was not the best way to cure his headache. __
10. Joan **intimidated** me with her nose. __
11. George **crept** into the room. Then he crept behind the crowd of people who were singing along with the piano player and stuffed his pockets with crackers and cheese, assorted veggies, some salami, and a banana nut muffin. George had lost his job two weeks earlier. __
12. Then, **at the drop of a hat**, George left the party, smiling at the late-arriving guests as he walked hurriedly out of the room. __

Practice 104: Do these make sense, or not?

Directions: If the information in the sentence is consistent, if everything fits OK, if there are no contradictions, nothing improbable or impossible, then write YES in the blank. However, if the parts don't fit, if it doesn't make sense, if its ridiculous or absurd, then write NO in the blank.

1. The dark **visions** of the misanthropes of this world are constructive. __
2. I guess you could say that Pam's suggestion was **constructive**. After all, it wouldn't hurt if every poor family had a jar of Persian caviar in their refrigerator. __
3. The **coarse** path was quite smooth. __
4. Frogs are **fascinating** to a little boy. __
5. Sam depended on her, but he had no **attachment** to her. __
6. They found the old man **wandering** around in the streets. __
7. The child who had fallen off her bike was sitting on the sidewalk **moaning**. __
8. The baby was pretty **fierce**. __
9. Jealousy is **amusing**. __
10. On every trip they took, Ken's wife **whined** about the car having no air-conditioning. That wasn't the case on the last trip. Ken had broken all the car windows. She had plenty of air. __
11. The Corvette **crept** along the freeway at 110 miles per hour. __
12. The sign said, "No **snails** on **stage**." __
13. Bobby's room was a **mess**, so we cleaned it up. __
14. Kim cries **at the drop of a hat** these days. She can't help it. She's going to have her first baby in six months. __
15. Before she would marry him, Jim had to take an **oath** to defend her cat. __
16. The old man was very **critical** of his wife. He kept telling her how gifted she was. __
17. Whenever I want **realism**, I go to a Walt Disney movie. __
18. Gary is very **ambitious**. He's working two jobs now while he's finishing up his Business degree. __
19. Charlie tried to beat up Cindy's old boyfriend because Charlie was **jealous**, but Cindy's old boyfriend beat the hell out of Charlie. It doesn't pay to be jealous. __
20. The next time, Charlie brought along his puppy to **intimidate** Cindy's old boyfriend. __

Really?

Directions: Explain your answers to these items:

2. _____
5. _____
8. _____
9. _____
12. _____
15. _____

Write

Directions: Write a sentence of your own for each of the words you are learning. Do not write sentences for words you already know. Instead, write a sentence for any substitute words you have chosen to learn.

Lesson 15 Study Guide

Word	Substitute	Similar	Opposite	Memory	✓
criticize					
a mess					
constructive					
moan					
whine					
dark visions					
fascinating					
attachment					
wander					
at the drop of a hat					
realism					
stage					
creep					
snail					
oath					
amusing					
jealousy					
ambition					
coarse					
fierce					
intimidate					

Gary is such a coward that he is intimidated by a snail.

Lesson 16 Focus Sheet

Word	✔	Subst Word	Listen	Speak	Read	Write
pursue						
quarrel						
endanger						
survive						
accumulate						
cautious						
tasty						
trim						
content						
slippers						
hose						
bass						
treble						
pouch						
whistle						
to come full circle						
sans						
oblivion						
tragedy						
routine						
uncertain						
significance						

Lesson 16

289. pursue /pər.su/ v.

Other forms: **pursuit** /pər.sut/ n. (-ed/-ing adj)
Meaning: If you pursue somebody, you go after him, you chase after him, you try to get him, you try to catch him.

Example:
The police pursued the drug dealer until they found him hiding in a dark alley inside a garbage can. He was in the right place.

Example:
A man pursues a woman until she catches him.

290. quarrel /kwar.əl/ v.

Other forms: **quarrel** /kwar.əl/ n. **quarreling** /kwarl.ɪŋ/ n/adj.
Opposite: friendly conversation
Meaning: When two people quarrel, they argue, they fight (with words), they have a disagreement.

Example:
The husband and wife quarreled with each other until the neighbor threw a brick through their bedroom window. Then they both quarreled with the neighbor about whether their quarreling was too loud or not.

Example:
It began with a quarrel. It ended with Doris standing over her dead husband, holding the smoking pistol in her right hand. Another advertisement for having guns in the house.

Tip 237: **pistol** = gun = handgun

291. endanger /ɛn.den.jər/ v.

Other forms: **dangerous** /den.jər.əs/ adj. **danger** /den.jər/ n. (-ly adv)
Opposite: make safe
Meaning: To endanger someone means to put that person in danger, to put that person in a dangerous situation which could harm him, injure him, even kill him.

Example:
Sally endangered her children by letting them play in the busy street.

Example:
By talking about the boss behind his back, Norm not only endangered his chances for a promotion, he also put his career in danger.

292. survive /sər.vaiv/ v.

Other forms: **survival** /sər.vaiv.əl/ n. **surviving** /sər.vai.vɪŋ/ adj.
Opposite: die
Meaning: If you survive, you stay alive or remain alive after a difficult or dangerous experience.

Example:
It was what you would call a good plane crash. All the passengers survived except the guy who was selling guns in developing countries.

Example:
Frances survived the test. Now all she had to do was finish her research paper on time.

293. accumulate /ə.kyum.yu.let/ v.

Other forms: **accumulation** /ə.kyum.yu.le.shən/ n. (-ed/-ing adj)
Opposite: throw away
Meaning: To accumulate things means to collect things, and the number of things you collect keeps growing and growing and growing until there's no more room in your garage.

Example:
Some people must believe that accumulation is the purpose of life. I saw a bumper sticker yesterday morning which read, "He who dies with the most toys wins."

Example:
Lester was a collector. Before he was fifty years old, he had already accumulated 10,189 baseball cards, 20,452 bottle tops, 12,333 gold coins, 57,558 stamps, 161,996 marbles, and 3 wives.

Tip 238: bumper sticker = a sign on the back of a car (on the bumper)

294. cautious /kɔ.shəs/ adj.

Other forms: **caution** /kɔ.shən/ n. (-ly adv)
Opposite: careless
Meaning: If you're cautious, you're careful.

Example:
Gary was very cautious with money. For example, he never paid for dinner when he went out with his friends, but he thought he had a good reason. He wanted to show them how to save money.

Example:
Alice was very cautious with men after Peter failed to show up for their wedding. She heard later that he had taken some blond to California.

295. tasty /tes.ti/ adj.

Other forms: **taste** /test/ v. **taste** /test/ n.
Opposite: Bleck! This tastes terrible.
Meaning: If something is tasty, it tastes good. You just love to eat it.

Example:
"That was a very tasty meal," the red back spider said of her recently departed husband.

Tip 239: Female red back spiders eat their mates during intercourse.
Tip 240: **intercourse** = making love
Tip 241: **departed** = left = gone

296. trim /trɪm/ v.

Other forms: **trimmed** /trɪmd/ adj.
Opposite: Don't cut it.
Meaning: To trim means to cut a little bit off.

Example:
When Hank, the former rock musician, decided to stop making music and start making money, he bought a suit, got a haircut and trimmed his beard.

Example:
Mrs. Lovato told Ronnie to go to the barber shop and get his hair trimmed. When he got home, Mrs. Lovato saw that Ronnie had no hair.
Mrs. Lovato: Ronnie, I thought I told you to get your hair trimmed.
Ronnie: I did, mom. I told the barber to trim my hair, like you said.
Mrs. Lovato: So why did you come home a skin head?
Ronnie: Well, the barber just kept trimming and trimming and trimming.

297. content /kən.tɛnt/ adj.

Other forms: **contented** /kən.tɛn.təd/ adj. **contentment** /kən.tɛnt.mənt/ n.
Opposite: not satisfied
Meaning: If you are content, you are satisfied with things the way they are.

Example:
Laura was filled with contentment watching her husband working in the garden as she rocked her baby girl in the rocking chair.

Example:
Bill Gates was content with the money he had made. Wouldn't you be content with $14,000,000,000 in the bank?

298. slippers /slɪ.pərz/ n. (plural)

Meaning: Slippers are like shoes, but they are worn inside the house, not outside. You cannot be a real grandfather or grandmother without them.

Example:
Maude came down the stairs in her curlers, her old pink robe and her bright green slippers and asked the guests, who were in evening gowns and tuxedos for the formal dinner party, if anyone had seen her teeth.

Tip 242: **curlers** = plastic devices for curling one's hair
Tip 243: **robe** = an indoor coat
Tip 244: **tuxedo** = a formal suit worn by men at weddings, formal dances, etc.

299. hose /hoz/ n.

Meaning: Hose and stockings are about the same, except that hose is a non-count noun (no plural form) and stockings is a count noun.

Example:
He watched her as she took off her hose, and was very glad she was his wife.

Example:
Just before she walked into the meeting, Sarah caught her hose on the corner of the copy machine, creating a seven inch run.

Tip 245: **She had a run in her hose.** = She had a hole in her stocking.

300. bass /bes/ n.

Meaning: Bass tones are low tones. A bass is a string instrument that produces low tones.

Example:
His voice echoed the tone of the bass player's melody as he read the poem to the coffee house audience.

301. treble /trɛ.bəl/ adj.

Opposite: bass
Meaning: Treble refers to high pitched sounds.

Example:
The 93-year-old actor spoke in a high treble, but the voice he heard was the young man's bass he had had when he was on stage in New York 30 years before.

302. pouch /pauch/ n.

Meaning: A pouch was usually a somewhat long, narrow leather bag that people kept their money in, in the old days.

Example:
The old man put his pouch in his pocket and left the house for the market.

303. whistle /wɪ.səl/ n.

Other forms: **whistle** /wɪ.səl/ v. **whistling** /wɪ.səl.ɪŋ/ adj.
Meaning: A whistle is a high pitched sound that is formed when air is forced through a very small opening.

Example:
Charles whistled as he spoke through the holes left by his missing teeth.

Example:
The teapot whistled on the stove as Barbara fixed the scrambled eggs for the boys.

304. to come full circle /sər.kəl/ Idiom

Meaning: To come full circle means to go back to the beginning or to repeat a pattern.

Example:
Victor's life had come full circle and he was content with what he had done. He faced his imminent death with no regrets, especially since he wasn't leaving a damn' dime to his ex-wife.

Example:
Things have come full circle. Manny is now supporting his father, who is at the university working towards a degree in Journalism. Thirty years ago, when Manny was at the university, his father supported him.

Tip 246: **imminent** = going to happen very soon

305. sans /sanz/ Preposition

Opposite: with
Meaning: Sans is a word we borrowed from the French (stole is a better word, since we're not giving it back). It means *without*.

Example:
The old man lay there near the fence in the refugee camp, dying - sans eyes, sans teeth, sans everything.

Example:
As the intimidating politician walked under the balcony towards the TV studio, a young man reached down from the balcony with a wire coat hanger and quickly lifted the politician's hair piece from atop his head. Shortly after, when the politician appeared in front of the TV cameras, he was far less intimidating *sans toupee*.

Tip 247: **sans toupee** = without his hair piece

306. oblivion /ə.blɪv.i.ən/ n.

Meaning: Oblivion refers to a state of nothingness.

Example:
The UN Peace keeper stepped on the land mine and was blown to oblivion.

Example:
Eddie, who was told last Tuesday that he has one month to live, believes that when we die that's it, that's the end, that's all she wrote. No heaven. No reincarnation. Dust to dust. Now, every day, he faces oblivion.

307. tragedy /træ.jə.di/ n.

Other forms: **tragic** /træ.jik/ adj.   **tragically** /træ.jik.li/ adv.
Opposite: comedy
Meaning: When a terrible event occurs, we call it a tragedy. Tragedy implies pain and suffering. A tragic story has a painfully unhappy ending.

Example:
It was a great tragedy for her. My loud, talkative wife had lost her voice.

Example:
They lived through a tragic marriage. For forty years, their affection for one another was smothered by disagreements over small things to such a degree that they could never get connected. Maybe there's a connection now. There's no sign of disagreement in the air as they lie close together in the soft grass of the cemetery.

Tip 248: **talkative** = She talks a lot.
Tip 249: **genuine** = real
Tip 250: **smother** = prevent someone from breathing

308. routine /ru.tin/ n.

Other forms: **routinely** /ru.tin.li/ adv.
Opposite: unusual behavior
Meaning: Our routines are those things we do every day or those things we do repeatedly in various situations. Routine behavior is habitual behavior. Routines are habits.

Example:
Every morning, Rodney followed the same routine. After getting dressed, going to the bathroom, brushing his teeth, shaving, and combing his hair, he would go down to the kitchen for breakfast, where he would have one egg, sunny side up, one strip of bacon, one slice of toast, and one cup of coffee. When he finished breakfast, he would put on his coat, his hat, and his scarf and walk to the front door. He would turn and kiss his wife on one cheek, always the right cheek, walk to the car, and drive away to work.

Tip 251: **eggs, sunny side up** = eggs fried on one side only
Tip 252: **scarf** = a piece of clothing worn around the neck to keep us warm

309. uncertain /ən.sər.tən/ adj.

Other forms: **uncertainty** /ən.sər.tən.ti/ n.
Opposite: sure
Meaning: Uncertain means not sure.

Example:
Sherry is uncertain about where she's going to go to college. She might go to MIT or she might go to Harvard or Stanford.

Example:
Paul lived a life of uncertainty. You never knew what he was going to do next.

310. significance /sɪg.nɪf.ə.kəns/ n.

Other forms: **significant** /sɪg.nɪf.ə.kənt/ adj. (-ly adv)
Opposite: unimportance
Meaning: Anything that is significant is important. If something has significance, it has importance or meaning for someone.

Example:
There was no significance to her remarks. Don't take them seriously. She was just having a bad hair day.

Practice 105 : Stress test

Directions : Underline the loudest syllable.

1. pursue 2. quarrel 3. endanger 4. survive
5. accumulate 6. cautious 7. tasty 8. content 9. slippers
10. treble 11. whistle 12. oblivion 13. tragedy 14. routine
15. uncertain 16. significance

Practice 106 : Stickers

Directions : Write a sticker from a story or example in the book that will help you remember what each word means. Cross out the words you already know and concentrate on those you don't.

Example: tasty: redback spider

1. pursue: _____
2. quarrel : _____
3. endanger : _____
4. survive : _____
5. accumulate : _____
6. cautious : _____
7. tasty : _____
8. trim : _____
9. content : _____
10. slippers : _____
11. hose : _____
12. bass : _____
13. treble : _____
14. pouch : _____
15. whistle : _____
16. come full circle : _____
17. sans : _____
18. oblivion : _____
19. tragedy : _____
20. routine : _____
21. uncertain : _____
22. significance : _____

Practice 107 : Using Your Own Experience

Directions : Write your own "story" and memory label to help you remember these words. If you already know a word, you don't need a Memory Label, of course, so write stories or examples only for those words you have trouble with.

1. pursue :

2. quarrel :

3. endanger :

4. survive :

5. accumulate :

6. cautious :

7. tasty :

8. trim :

9. content :

10. slippers :

11. hose :

12. bass :

13. treble :

14. pouch :

15. whistle :
_____
_____
16. come full circle :
_____
_____
17. sans :
_____
_____
18. oblivion :
_____
_____
19. tragedy :
_____
_____
20. routine :
_____
_____
21. uncertain :
_____
_____
22. significance :
_____
_____

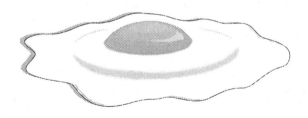

One egg, sunny side up.

Practice 108 : Simple Connections

Directions : Choose a word that <u>suggests</u> the meaning of the boldfaced word. Put the appropriate letter in the blank.

a. not sure **b.** argue **c.** dangerous **d.** alive **e.** get **f.** careful **g.** love it
h. cut **i.** satisfied **j.** inside **k.** stockings **l.** low **m.** bag **n.** high **o.** blow
p. back to beginning **q.** without **r.** nothingness **s.** terrible **t.** ordinary
u. go after **v.** importance

1. **Pursue** your dreams. Nobody else will. __
2. John was pretty **trim** after dieting and working out for six months. __
3. Gus **accumulated** a lot of money and many friends over the years. __
4. Randy turned up the **treble** so high you couldn't hear the drums. __
5. The explosives blew the bus, its innocent passengers and the suicide bomber to **oblivion**. __
6. They never paid much attention to Fred, for what he said usually had little **significance**. __
7. Allowing farmers to continue to use that pesticide **endangers** farm workers and those living near the farms. __
8. I was always a little **cautious** around the snacks my Chinese wife brought with her on our trips. Perhaps it was because she called them snakes. __
9. Whenever Eben's 1964 Dodge Dart got low on gas, he would turn the **bass** on his stereo system all the way up and the car would bounce to his destination. __
10. Losing all his money in the poker game was a minor **tragedy**. __
11. As Walt listened to his voice calling on his wife to bring him some coffee, he was reminded of the treble of his boyhood. Indeed, his life had **come full circle**. __
12. Sally and Dan **quarreled** into the night over family finances. __
13. ---
   <u>Gary</u>: Are the **slippers** tasty?
   <u>Gary's dog</u> : Mrrruph Mrrruph. Grrraugh mun uh. (Yes, excellent. Care to try some?) __
14. The fate of Gary's dog is **uncertain**. __
15. The spareribs Susan was eating were quite **tasty**, but she didn't look too feminine with all that barbecue sauce on her face. __
16. Gladys anxiously stretched the **hose** onto her long legs, put on her slip, guided the dress over her lovely shoulders, put on her shoes, and answered the door, only to be greeted by a soap salesman. __
17. She went to the door **sans** makeup. __
18. ---
<u>Sarah</u>: How are you these days?
<u>Sam</u>: Oh, same old **routine**. School, work, homework, sleep.
<u>Sarah</u> : Why don't you take a break and go to the beach with us tomorrow? __

19. —
> **Sam**: Maybe I could. I can take my book and **whistle** at the women between chapters. __

20. Eilis doesn't know how she is going to **survive** these frustrating, confusing years as a young adult. And her Dad is no help. When she asked him the other day what would help, all he said was "time passes." __

21. Little Lenny had a **pouch** filled with marbles that he said was worth at least $1,000. __

22. Jerry was **content** with his job until the opportunity for a promotion opened up. __

A tragic philosophy.

Practice 109 : Similarities

<u>Directions</u> : Write a word in each blank which is related to this word.

1. depart : _____   _____

Practice 110 : Opposites

<u>Directions</u> : Choose a word that means the opposite of the boldfaced word. Put the appropriate letter in the blank.

a. keep safe **b.** die **c.** throw away **d.** careless **e.** don't cut it
f. not satisfied **g.** progressed **h.** unusual **i.** positive **j.** unimportant

1. When Jerry knew there was a chance to get a better paying position, he was no longer **content** with the job he had. __
2. After thinking about the new position for a week, Jerry began to feel he couldn't **survive** in his current position. __
3. Strange, isn't it. Jerry was perfectly content with his current **routine** until he got a taste of greater possibilities. __
4. When he learned that he didn't get the promotion, he was depressed for a while, but he eventually realized that the job he has is just fine. Good ol' Jerry had **come full circle**. __
5. Jerry was not **uncertain** about how he would handle the next promotional opportunity. __
6. Joe was very **cautious** around the O'Brien's bulldog. The dog never barked and never growled, but Joe knew it was waiting for an opportunity. __
7. We need to **trim** the marketing budget by 20%. __
8. We have **accumulated** too many on-going advertising expenses and sales are not rising. __
9. Guns **endanger** the lives of the people around them. __
10. "I **comprehend** everything you have said," said the professor. "Unfortunately, it has no significance." __

Practice 111: Do these make sense, or not?

Directions: If the information in the sentence is consistent, if everything fits OK, if there are no contradictions, nothing improbable or impossible, then write YES in the blank. However, if the parts don't fit, if it doesn't make sense, if its ridiculous or absurd, then write NO in the blank.

1. Greg is a little **cautious**. He always wipes the doorknob with a handkerchief before he opens a door. __
2. I betcha (bet you) we'll find a lot of fascinating things in **oblivion**. __
3. I didn't worry about it because it had no **significance**. __
4. It's easy to **accumulate** a lot of money if you are overly cautious. __
5. Steve has an almost feminine **treble** voice. __
6. Nancy had no trouble understanding him on the phone because he was **sans** teeth. __
7. After the argument was over, they **quarreled** for another two hours. __
8. The oppressive heat **endangered** the lives of the old couple that lived in the boarding house because it had air-conditioning. __
9. It is **routine** for politicians to kiss babies. __
10. Eben turned the **bass** up so much it blew holes in her **hose**. __
11. Stan **pursued** the thief, but he didn't follow him. __
12. Stevie hated every minute of it as his mother **trimmed** his hair for his two-year-old birthday party. __
13. Sue was **content** to stand there freezing in the doorway. __
14. Pete was **uncertain** whether the **whistle** worked or nor, so he blew it. The only problem with that was that it was 4 o'clock in the morning and his parents were sleeping in the next room. Pete is lucky he is still alive. __
15. On that blistering hot day as she struggled with the groceries and her five-month-old son, Shirley thought it was a **tragedy** that human mothers didn't have **pouches** like kangaroos. __
16. They sat down to a **tasty** meal of bread and water. __
17. Slow sales followed by a relatively long period of booming sales, succeeded by slow sales. Harry's business had **come full circle**. __
18. **Slippers** are worn on the ears. __
19. Roy did not **survive**, but at least he was still alive. __

Really?
Directions: Explain your answers to these items :

1. _____
2. _____
7. _____
13. _____

Write

Directions: Write a sentence of your own for each of the words you are learning. Do not write sentences for words you already know. Instead, write a sentence for any substitute words you have chosen to learn.

Lesson 16 Study Guide

Word	Substitute	Similar	Opposite	Memory	✓
pursue					
quarrel					
endanger					
survive					
accumulate					
cautious					
tasty					
trim					
content					
slippers					
hose					
bass					
treble					
pouch					
whistle					
to come full circle					
sans					
oblivion					
tragedy					
routine					
uncertain					
significance					

Being a fly can endanger one's life.

Index

A series of 176
abruptly 100
Absolutely not! 32
accumulate 267
actor 225
additionally 101
adolescent 64
all of a sudden 163
alternative 178
although 19
amateur 34
ambition 251
amusing 250
an exception to the rule 8
ancient 157
angular 181
anxious 49
artistic 7
astronomy 192
at the drop of a hat 248
at the turn of the century 178
attachment 247
avant guarde 50

Bass 269
bathe 125
beak 209
bear something in mind 160
blissful 102
boarding school 8
boredom 52

Cautious 267
century 163
chaos 158
charcoal 124
circular 181
circumstances 227
coarse 252
coherent 196
compound 195
comprehend 196
concentric 177
conclude 122
condense 192
condolences 81
confined 230
conflicting views 210
confusion 157
conserve 180
considerable 63
constantly 7
constructive 245
content 268
cool 194
corn husk 136
cowardice 230
creation 159
creativity 66
creep 249
criticize 244
curious 17
current 161
cynic 230

Dark visions 246
delighted 36
demand 212
dense 177
deprivation 103
diagonal 123
dignity 139
disciplined 6
disguised 33
dishonest 207
disk-shaped 176
disorderly 36
distrust 231
disturbing 225
dominance 67
dramatic 85
drew 8
duplicate 163
dust 161

Elder 158
emergence 106
encourage 20
endanger 266
enthusiastic 7
equivalent 164
Eros 158
even more 101
eventual 211
evident 88
evolve 17
excel 16
excessive 20
expectation 229
extraordinarily 65
extremely 65
extroversion 67

Failure 231
fascinating 246
feast 120
fictitious 138
fierce 252
filibuster 100
foolish 69
forbidden 101
foreign 122
frightening 83
fundamental 47
funeral 82
furious 224
furthermore 100

Gaseous 193
genetics 226
genius 4
gesture 225
giant 21
gifted 3
give comfort to someone 232
Goddess 137
grain 195
gravitational 164
greedy 48

grow 213
guts 68

Handle with kid gloves 6
hardship 139
harsh 141
have a lump in your throat 176
healed 119
heavenly body 162
hero 36
heroine 36
hippie 51
hooked on something 32
horizontal 123
hose 269
humanity 212
humiliated 105

Identify with 107
ignorance 161
impress upon 140
in a rut 229
in addition 100
incorporation 119
inevitable 211
infamous 35
infancy 81
infected 124
infinite 211
insect 18
intense 49
interpret 227
intimidate 253
inward 180
irresistible 33
isolation 86
It's settled 31

Jealousy 251
judgment 142

K no entries

Lifeless 106

loft 5
long for something 50

Mask 121
massage 137
maturation 85
meaningless 224
mental 50
mess 244
misanthrope 213
miserable 224
moan 245
momentum 181
monk 209
moody 5
moreover 100
most likely 64
motivate 37
mythical 136

Naturalist 18
navel 123
nebulous 165
Never in a million years! 32
nonconformity 66
Not for all the tea in China! 32
Not on your life! 32

Oath 250
obedient 16
oblivion 271
obsessed 209
on a single occasion 87
On the one hand. 213
on the other hand 213

oppressive 141
optimal 51
ordeal 105
origin 87
oxymoron 191

Parachute 34
paradox 191

particularly 64
pattern 63
photographer 208
pinch 104
point of view 224
popularize 68
potential 3
pouch 270
previous 35
primary 142
probable 179
productive 118
projector 17
prosecution 46
prototype 192
pull something off 35
puppet 227
pursue 266

Quarrel 266

Radiate 194
range from X to Y 17
razor 123
realism 248
reasonable 65
reinforce 138
rejection 140
relearn 121
relieve 84
remarkably 65
renew 118
repetition 62
reveal 121
risky 49
rite 81
ritual 82
role 84
routine 272

Sacred 105
sans 270
seek 47
sensation 47

shrink, shrank, shrunk 180
shy 20
significance 272
similarity 137
skater 182
slippers 269
snail 250
solar 178
soldier 19
solidarity 118
spectrum 86
sphere 194
spin 182
split up 196
stage 249
status 120
storm out 195
stressful 83
studio 6
stunt 46
subtle 86
sue for damages 36
survive 267
swinger 51
symbolic 103
sympathetic 16

Tasty 268
telescope 159
temperamental 4
tend to 63
theorize 48
thermal 193
threaten 143
thrill 46
to be half right 195
to beat around the bush 208
to coin 88
to come full circle 270
to cry over spilled milk 228
to fast 103
to jump to conclusions 19
to make a fortune 210
to perfect 213

To put it bluntly 207
to settle for less 228
to string 34
To tell the truth 208
tragedy 271
transformation 88
transition 83
trapped 179
treble 269
trim 268

Uncertain 272
unethical 212
unique 178
unusually 65

Variety 62
vertical 123
vigorous 137
vitality 142
vortex 162

Wander 247
whine 245
whirling and twirling 182
whistle 270
white water rafting 31

X accounts for Y 140
X could be described as Y 160

Yank 104

Z no entries